2024 Travel Guide to Bologna

to Bologna

Exploring the Food Scene: The Perfect Pickled Blend of Seasonello Aromatic Spices in Bologna. Discovering Lebanon's Herbal Salt

Rick Paul

Disclaimer Notice

Journey Through Aromatic Flavors

In the heart of Italy, I embarked on a journey that forever changed my perspective on travel. Bologna, with its rich history, culinary delights, and vibrant culture, became my sanctuary. I reveled in the taste of pickled Bologna, marveled at the intricate flavors of Lebanon's herbal salt, and explored the city's aromatic markets.

But my adventure in Bologna was more than just personal enrichment; it was a desire to make travel accessible to all. This book is my way of sharing the secrets of this enchanting city, to ensure that future travelers can experience its wonders without barriers.

I want others to feel the same sense of awe that I did as they navigate the bustling streets, savor the local cuisine, and immerse themselves in the beauty of Bologna. Join me in this book as we unlock the doors to this remarkable destination, making the magic of Bologna attainable for all who dream of wandering its charming streets.

Contents

An Overview of Bologna

As a seasoned traveler, I've explored the bustling streets of several cities, marveled at architectural marvels, and sampled the cuisines of many civilizations. Among all of my travels, one city in particular has left an unforgettable imprint on my soul: Bologna, Italy.

It was a chance encounter that took me to this lovely location. Arriving in Bologna with a sense of amazement and curiosity, I was immediately charmed by the city's timeless appeal. The warm ochre colors of historic buildings, the symphony of church bells resounding through small alleyways, and the aroma of freshly baked bread wafting from local bakeries all greeted me with open arms.

My days were spent exploring Piazza Maggiore's grandeur, where the imposing Palazzo Comunale stood as a tribute to Bologna's rich history. As I climbed the Asinelli Tower, I took in the panoramic perspective of the city, realizing that every corner had a story to tell. The Basilica of San Petronio rose tall, embellished with artistic marvels that appeared to speak of bygone periods.

I discovered secret courtyards decked with blossoming flowers and calm sanctuaries that offered respite from the world's hectic pace as I traveled further into the city's convoluted alleyways. Bologna's Archiginnasio, with its grand staircase and old library, instilled in me awe and veneration for the pursuit of knowledge.

My time in Bologna was distinguished by more than simply majestic landmarks. It was the interactions with the locals, the laughing at crowded osterias, and the delight of discovering a busy street fair that made this journey genuinely memorable. The people of Bologna were friendly and welcoming, asking me to participate in their traditions and enjoy the simple pleasures of life.

In this trip guide, I wish to share the essence of Bologna with you. I took notes, acquired thoughts, and recorded every element that made my experience remarkable as I journeyed through this wonderful city. I felt impelled to establish a resource that would help fellow travelers navigate the charming streets of Bologna, appreciate its culinary riches, and immerse themselves in its lively culture.

Not only will you discover important information on these pages, but you'll also get a peek into the essence of Bologna, a city that dances between the past and the present, where art, music, and gastronomy mix to create a tapestry of magic. I invite you to join me as we explore the city's neighborhoods, discover hidden treasures, and experience the festivals that fill the calendar with color and excitement.

With this travel guide in hand, my aim is that you, too, will be enchanted by Bologna, and that you will keep the city's soul with you long after you leave. I'm pleased to share this journey with you and open the doors to the enchanting world of Bologna, a city that welcomes its guests with a warm embrace and an invitation to explore its timeless beauties, whether you're a seasoned traveler or embarking on your first voyage.

So, let us embark on our journey through the heart of Italy, where the soul of Bologna awaits to embrace you in its eternal charm.

1.1. Hello and welcome to Bologna.

Welcome to Bologna, a captivating city where history, culture, and gastronomic delights join together to create a unique experience. As you arrive, prepare to be fascinated by the distinct character and warm warmth of this charming Italian town.

The Heart of Emilia-Romagna

Bologna, in the Emilia-Romagna region of northern Italy, is a city with a rich tapestry of legacy. It is well-known for its medieval architecture, red-colored houses, and the distinctive porticos that run along the streets, offering shade from both rain and sun.

A Training Facility

Bologna is the proud home of the world's oldest institution, the Bologna institution, founded in 1088. Throughout history, this university has had a significant impact on the city's cultural and intellectual life, earning Bologna the nickname "la dotta" (the learned).

The Towers of Bologna

As you visit the city, you'll see a pair of leaning buildings on the skyline - the Two structures (Due Torri). The Asinelli Tower and the Garisenda Tower are Bologna landmarks that offer panoramic views of the city from their heights. For the daring visitor, climbing the Asinelli Tower is a must-do adventure.

Gastronomic Delights

Bologna is an epicurean haven, and foodies will be in heaven. The city is known and appreciated around the world for its scrumptious cuisine, particularly the thick and savory Bolognese sauce served with tagliatelle. Visit local trattorias and osterias to get a true taste of Bologna.

Art and culture

Bologna, being a historical city, is a treasure trove of art and culture. The historic centre is a UNESCO World Heritage site, brimming with architectural marvels and hidden gems. History pervades every corner and cranny, from the majestic Basilica di San Petronio to the old Archiginnasio, where the university used to hold lectures.

A pleasant and warm atmosphere

Beyond the architectural marvels and delectable cuisine, the people of Bologna truly differentiate the city. The locals, known as "Bolognesi," are eager to share their love for their city with you. Don't be surprised if you find yourself immersed in delightful Bolognese conversations, whether in a café or while strolling through the colorful markets.

Festivals and Events that are Exciting

Throughout the year, Bologna comes alive with thrilling festivals and events that celebrate art, music, and culture.

From the bright street performances of the "Estate Felsinea" summer festival to the cinematic delights of the "Biografilm Festival," the city is always buzzing with activity.

Location of Exploration in Bologna

Because of its strategic location, Bologna is an excellent starting point for visiting Emilia-Romagna and beyond. Thanks to its well-connected transit links, you can easily travel on day trips to other fascinating cities such as Florence, Venice, and Ravenna, each of which offers diverse experiences.

As you enter Bologna's wonderful world, prepare to be captivated by its history, charmed by its culture, and seduced by its gourmet treasures. Whether you enjoy art, history, food, or simply want to immerse yourself in Italian beauty, Bologna has something for you. Enjoy your excursion through Emilia-Romagna's heart, and let the city's warm embrace leave an indelible impression on your heart.

1.2. A Brief History of Bologna

We'll go back in time to learn about the fascinating history of Bologna, a city that has seen centuries of triumphs, challenges, and cultural achievements.

History of the Etruscans and the Romans

Bologna is a city with a lengthy history. It was founded by the Etruscans about the sixth century BC and was known as "Felsina." Later, during the Roman era, the city gained significance as "Bononia," becoming an important center for trade and commerce due to its strategic location along the Roman route, Via Aemilia.

The Glorious Age of Medieval Times

Bologna experienced a watershed point during the Middle Ages. During the 11th and 12th centuries, the city experienced population growth and economic progress, establishing itself as a prominent center of learning and culture. Bologna University was founded in 1088, making it the world's oldest institution continuing in operation today. This prestigious institution attracted intellectuals from all over Europe, gaining Bologna the nickname "la dotta" (the learned).

Towers and Nobility

Multiple towers dominated Bologna's skyline during the medieval period, symbolizing the authority and wealth of strong families. The city had around 180 towers at its peak. The Asinelli Tower and the Garisenda Tower are notable reminders of this era. These towers served as defenses, status symbols, and observation posts.

Renaissance and Expansion of the Arts

During the Renaissance period, Bologna had significant cultural and artistic achievements. Nicola Pisano and Jacopo della Quercia, to name a few, made their mark on the city's architecture and sculptures. Notably, the magnificent Basilica di San Petronio began building during this time period, paying homage to Bologna's cultural splendor.

Papal Rule and Unification

In the 16th century, the Papal States reigned over Bologna. During this time, the city saw both political and aesthetic revolutions, with the Catholic Church's influence directing its development. Bologna remained under papal rule until the nineteenth century, when Italy was unified, and in 1860, it became a province of the Kingdom of Italy.

Bologna in the present day

Throughout the twentieth century, Bologna saw industrialization and expansion. The city developed into a significant industrial center, contributing to Italy's economic growth. It did, however, face challenges such as WWII destruction and urbanization, which altered its landscape. Despite these changes, Bologna has managed to preserve its old heritage, and the city's efforts to preserve its cultural treasures were recognized when the historic center was designated a UNESCO World Heritage Site.

In the Present, Bologna

Bologna is a vibrant and dynamic city that celebrates its rich heritage while still looking ahead. Its thriving university, cultural activities, and culinary prowess continue to draw visitors from all over the world. The history of Bologna is woven into the fabric of its streets, buildings, and traditions, providing visitors with an authentic and immersive contact with the heart of Italy's cultural legacy.

While exploring Bologna's medieval streets, keep in mind the varied stories of the people who walked these paths centuries ago. Every corner and crevice holds a piece of history ready to be discovered and cherished. Embrace "la dotta" culture and allow Bologna's heritage to enchant you as you create your own memories in this timeless city.

1.3. The Cultural Importance of Bologna

Bologna, nicknamed "la dotta" (the learned), has a rich cultural past that has left an indelible mark on the world. From its historic university to its creative accomplishments, the city's contributions have shaped Italy's cultural milieu.

The Oldest University in the World

One of the most important aspects of Bologna's cultural legacy is its great university. Bologna University, founded in 1088, is the world's oldest continually operating institution. It was critical in the development of higher education, establishing the groundwork for modern institutions worldwide. It once held great thinkers like Dante Alighieri and Nicolaus Copernicus. Today, the school continues to attract students and academics from a wide range of fields, continuing on a legacy of intellectual discovery and knowledge.

The Bolognese Painting School

The Bolognese School of Painting, which emerged during the Renaissance period, symbolizes the artistic achievements of Bologna. This art movement gave birth to well-known artists such as the Carracci family—Ludovico, Annibale, and Agostino—who influenced the development of Baroque and Neoclassical painting. Their innovative approach to art education, which emphasized drawing from life, anatomy studies, and nature observation, contributed to Bologna's reputation as a center of artistic excellence.

Archiginnasio and Anatomical Theater

A former university campus, the Archiginnasio, is a wonderful testament to Bologna's cultural past. It was constructed in the 16th century and once housed one of Europe's greatest libraries. It is a work of art in architecture, adorned with medieval coats of arms and sculptures. The Anatomical Theater, where medical students used to witness dissections, is open to visitors at the Archiginnasio. This theater offers a fascinating glimpse into the city's dedication to both science and the arts.

Culinary Capital of Italy

Bologna's cultural significance extends to its culinary legacy. As the capital of Emilia-Romagna, a region noted for its culinary delights, Bologna is a foodie's dream. Traditional dishes such as tagliatelle al ragù (Bolognese sauce), tortellini, mortadella, and parmigiano reggiano cheese have grown popular worldwide. The city's dedication to maintaining and developing unique recipes is reflected in the moniker "la grassa" (the fat one), which praises the city's savory culinary offerings.

Historic architecture and porticos

Bologna's architectural treasures strongly display the city's cultural past. The city's historic core, which comprises medieval and Renaissance structures, has been exceptionally well preserved. The Basilica di San Petronio and the Palazzo d'Accursio are two notable landmarks that surround the Piazza Maggiore, Bologna's core. Bologna's porticos, which span over 38 kilometers and form the world's longest covered walkway network, are one of the city's most unique architectural features. These porticos offer refuge from the weather as well as an excellent urban experience.

Festivals & Celebrations of the Past

Throughout the year, Bologna is alive with traditional festivals and events that highlight its cultural vibrancy. One of the most well-known celebrations is the "Festa di San Petronio," which honors the city's patron saint. During this occasion, the Piazza Maggiore hosts vibrant performances, parades, and concerts, attracting both locals and visitors.

Contemporary Art and Music Scenes

Bologna's cultural importance can still be felt today, with a vibrant modern art and music scene. Galleries, street art, and music venues all contribute to the city's artistic diversity. Film and music festivals such as "Biografilm Festival" and "Bologna Sonic Park" honor both film and music by allowing both new and seasoned artists to perform.

Bologna's cultural significance is woven into a tapestry of history, art, academia, and culinary delights that continue to shape the city's identity. When you immerse yourself in Bologna's cultural offerings, you will discover a city that values its heritage while embracing originality and innovation, a true testament to the depth and diversity of Italian culture.

1.4. Local customs and etiquette

Understanding and respecting local customs and etiquette will enhance your trip and ensure positive interactions with the friendly Bolognesi as you immerse yourself in Bologna's lively culture.

Interaction and greetings on a personal level

When meeting someone in Bologna, a pleasant greeting is expected. Italians frequently use a brief handshake or two cheek kisses when greeting acquaintances and relatives. Keeping eye contact during conversations shows interest and respect.

Punctuality and timing are essential.

Italians have a relaxed attitude regarding timing. While formal appointments are expected to start on time, social gatherings may start a little later. Accept the slow pace and enjoy the moment.

The Dress Regulations

Bologna is a stylish city where people dress elegantly. While there is no formal dress code, it is advised to avoid wearing anything too casual or exposing when visiting places like churches or sophisticated dining establishments.

Table Manners and Dining Etiquette

In Bologna, dining is a revered experience, and specific dining etiquettes are practiced. Keep the following in mind:

Reservations: To ensure a seat, it is traditional to make reservations, especially at popular restaurants.

Seating: If your table has been assigned, wait for the host or staff to escort you to it.

While bread is traditionally served without butter, olive oil and balsamic vinegar may be on the table. You can dip your bread in oil and vinegar if you want.

Pasta & Sauce: With the exception of pasta al forno (baked spaghetti), residents of Bologna frequently enjoy pasta dishes devoid of grated cheese.

Language and Communication

While Italian is the official language, many Bolognesi speak English, especially in tourist areas. Simple Italian expressions such as "buongiorno" (good morning) and "grazie" (thank you) will, nonetheless, be enthusiastically welcomed and appreciated.

Tipping

Tipping is less popular in Bologna than in other countries because service charges are typically included in restaurant bills. However, a small payment to indicate gratitude for excellent service is appreciated. You can round up the cost of living to the nearest 5% of the total sum.

Sacred Sites Must Be Protected

Bologna is home to numerous magnificent churches and cathedrals. To promote a respectful atmosphere, please dress modestly and talk quietly when visiting these sacred sites.

Public Behaviour

Bologna is a safe city, but like with any city, you should stay mindful of your valuables and surroundings. Avoid loud or disruptive behavior in public areas to express concern for others.

Manners on the Street

The historic streets of Bologna can become congested, particularly during busy tourist seasons. Keep an eye out for other pedestrians and avoid standing in the middle of narrow streets or in front of doorways.

Bargaining and Shopping

In Bologna, haggling is uncommon, especially in well-known businesses and boutiques. However, in open-air markets, you might gently inquire about pricing flexibility.

Saying Goodbye

When it's time to say goodbye, a simple "arrivederci" (goodbye) or "a presto" (see you soon) is a polite way to bid farewell to new friends or acquaintances.

By adhering to local customs and etiquette, you will discover that the people of Bologna will warmly welcome you, making your visit to this fascinating city even more enjoyable and rewarding.

Plan a Trip to Bologna

2.1. When Is the Most Appropriate Time to Visit Bologna?

Because each season has its own set of benefits and activities, visiting Bologna at the right time can have a significant impact on your experience. Here's a whole season breakdown to help you plan the perfect vacation:

The spring season (from March through May)

Spring is a great season to visit Bologna because the weather gradually warms up after the winter frost. During the day, temperatures range from 15°C to 20°C (59°F to 68°F), with intermittent rains. Mornings and evenings may still be cool, so dress in layers.

Advantages: Bologna's streets and parks come alive with vivid colors as flowers bloom throughout the city.

Mild Weather: Enjoy beautiful weather great for walking or biking around the city.

Fewer Crowds: Because spring has fewer people than summer, you can experience popular attractions with fewer lineups.

Festivals and other events:

Festa di San Petronio: On May 7, Bologna's patron saint's festival features processions, music, and cultural events that create a festive atmosphere across the city.

Summertime (June to August)

Summer temperatures in Bologna can range from 25°C to 30°C (77°F to 86°F), with heatwaves on occasion. Bring a sun hat and sunscreen to protect yourself from the heat on hot, sunny days.

Advantages

Bologna comes alive with outdoor concerts, fairs, and colorful street acts during the "Estate Felsinea" summer festival.

Al Fresco Dining: At Bologna's open-air cafés and restaurants, you may enjoy the pleasures of dining alfresco.

Summer days are longer, allowing you to spend more time exploring the city's attractions.

Considerations

Because summer is the peak tourist season, popular destinations may be crowded. To avoid huge queues, plan ahead of time and arrive early.

Heat and humidity: Monitor the temperature, especially throughout the day. Keep hydrated and take breaks in the shade as needed.

Festivals and other events

From June to September, Estate Felsinea hosts a summer festival in the city that includes a variety of cultural activities, concerts, and plays.

The fall season (September through November)

Weather: Autumn is a pleasant season in Bologna, with temperatures ranging from 15°C to 25°C (59°F to 77°F). The weather is frequently pleasant, making this an ideal time for outdoor activities.

Advantages:

The surrounding landscape transforms into a tapestry of autumn colors, providing nature aficionados with stunning views.

Autumn is the season for truffle fairs, wine festivals, and food festivals, each of which offers a one-of-a-kind culinary experience.

Wet Days: Although fall offers fewer wet days than spring, showers are still likely. Bring an umbrella or a light raincoat with you.

Festivals and other events:

Truffle Fairs: In September and October, truffle fairs such as the Fiera Nazionale del Tartufo Bianco in Savigno are held, where you may sample and purchase this prized delicacy.

Wine Festivals: Emilia-Romagna is famed for its wine, and autumn brings wine festivals where you may sample local vintages.

The winter season (from December through February)

Bologna's winters are cold and damp, with temperatures ranging from 0°C to 10°C (32°F to 50°F). Snow is unusual, although it is possible.

Advantages:

Bologna transforms into a winter wonderland during the Christmas season, filled with beautiful lights, markets, and decorations.

Lower Prices: Because January is considered the off-season for tourists, you may discover more affordable lodging and less crowds.

Because winter days offer less daylight hours, plan your outings accordingly.

Cool Temperatures: To stay warm on chilly days and evenings, bundle up and wear warmly.

Festivals and other events:

Christmas Markets: Immerse yourself in the enchanting atmosphere of Bologna's Christmas markets, such as the Mercato di Natale di Bologna, which sells seasonal delicacies and local goods.

By considering your preferences for weather, people, and seasonal activities, you can select the best time to visit Bologna and create a unique experience.

2.2. Recommendations for Stay Length

The length of your stay in Bologna depends on your interests, preferences, and level of exploration. Bologna has a wide range of historical, cultural, and culinary events to offer, so spending enough time there to immerse yourself in its unique environment is recommended. Here are some particular recommendations:

Stay for two to three days

Overview: A two to three-day vacation to Bologna allows you to experience the city's highlights and major attractions.

Recommendations:

Piazza Maggiore: In the heart of Bologna, visit the great Basilica di San Petronio and the historic Palazzo d'Accursio.

Climb the Asinelli Tower for panoramic views of the city, then meander around the Garisenda Tower.

Archiginnasio: Learn about Bologna's history by visiting this architectural marvel as well as the Anatomical Theater.

Local Cuisine: Sample Bologna's culinary delights, including a classic Bolognese lunch at a local osteria.

Stroll the charming portico-covered streets, uncovering hidden courtyards and gorgeous alleys.

Gelato: For authentic Italian gelato, go to one of Bologna's legendary gelaterias.

Moderate Stay (four to five days)

A medium stay of 4 to 5 days allows you to delve further into Bologna's history, art, and culture, as well as take day trips to nearby attractions.

Suggestions for Improvement:

Museums and Galleries: In Bologna, check out the National Art Gallery, the Archaeological Museum, and the Museum of Modern Art (MAMbo).

Santo Stefano Basilica: Visit the "Santo Stefano" complex of seven churches to learn about the city's religious history.

Day Trips: Learn more about the Emilia-Romagna region by visiting nearby cities such as Florence, Venice, Ravenna, or Modena.

Cooking class: Learn how to make pasta and other regional cuisines with a traditional cooking class.

Shopping: Look for one-of-a-kind souvenirs and products at local markets and stores.

Nightlife in Bologna is vibrant, with everything from aperitivo bars to live music venues and cultural activities.

Stay for an extended amount of time (at least one week)

Overview: Spending a week or more in Bologna allows you to immerse yourself in the city's cultural fabric and experience it as a local.

Suggestions for Improvement:

Visit the charming villages that surround Bologna, such as Dozza, Vignola, and Castelvetro, which are known for their historic charm and wine production.

Language and Culture: Learning Italian will allow you to interact with locals and extend your cultural experience.

Discover hidden gems by looking for local artisans, traditional workshops, and lesser-known locations.

Seasonal Events: Plan your trip around seasonal events like truffle fairs, wine festivals, or the "Estate Felsinea" summer festival for a more immersive experience.

Finally, how long you remain in Bologna is entirely up to you, and any amount of time will offer you with a rewarding experience in this wonderful Italian city. The more time you have, the more you will discover about its fascinating history, cultural legacy, and culinary delights.

2.3. Visas and Entry Requirements

When planning a trip to Bologna, be sure you have all of the necessary visas and admission criteria. The exact requirements will depend on your nationality and the purpose of your stay. Here's a step-by-step tutorial to get you started:

Visa to enter the Schengen Zone

Italy is a member of the Schengen Area, a group of European countries that have abolished internal border controls. If you are a citizen of a country that is not a member of the European Union (EU) or the European Free

Trade Association (EFTA), you may need to apply for a Schengen Visa to enter Italy.

Categories of Schengen Visa:

Tourist Visa (Type C): This visa is intended for sightseeing, tourism, and visiting family and friends.

Visit conferences or meetings with a business visa (Type C).

Type B Transit Visa: For short layovers in non-Schengen countries.

Travel Without a Visa

Citizens of certain countries are exempt from obtaining a Schengen Visa for short stays (up to 90 days within a 180-day period) for tourist, business, or family visits. This is known as visa-free entry.

Citizens of the EU, EFTA, and several other countries, including the United States, Canada, Australia, New Zealand, Japan, South Korea, and many others, are not required to obtain a visa to enter Italy for short stays.

Admission Requirements

Regardless of whether you need a visa, you must meet the following general entry requirements:

Passport: A passport that is valid for at least three months beyond your planned stay in Italy is required.

If you do not need a visa, you will receive an entry stamp in your passport indicating the date of admittance.

Long-Term Stay Visas and Residence Permits

If you plan to stay in Italy for more than 90 days for reasons such as studying, working, or visiting family, you must apply for a long-stay visa or residence card before you arrive.

Long-Term Visa Categories:

Study Visa (Type D): This visa is for students planning to study in Italian universities or educational institutes.

Work Visa (Type D): This visa is for people who have been offered work in Italy.

Family Reunion Visa (Type D): For family members of Italian or EU/EFTA nationalities.

The Visa Application Form

To apply for a Schengen Visa or a long-stay visa, you must contact the Italian embassy or consulate in your home country. The application procedure frequently includes the following steps:

Gather all relevant documentation, including a completed visa application form, passport photographs, trip insurance, proof of lodging, plane itinerary, and financial papers.

Schedule a meeting with the Italian embassy or consulate in your country.

During an interview at the embassy or consulate, you may be asked about the purpose of your visit and your travel plans.

Processing Time: Because visa processing timelines vary, apply well in advance of your planned travel dates.

Travel Protection Insurance

While in Italy, it is suggested that you purchase travel insurance that covers medical emergencies, trip cancellations, and other unforeseen circumstances.

Before planning your trip to Bologna, check the specific visa and entry requirements for your country and travel purpose. Make sure you have all of the necessary documents for a trouble-free trip to this picturesque Italian city.

2.4. Modes of Transportation (Air, Train, and Bus)

Bologna is well-connected to the rest of Italy and Europe, making it simple to travel there by aircraft, train, or bus. Here's a thorough explanation of the transportation options for your trip to and from Bologna:

Air travel is available.

Bologna Guglielmo Marconi Airport (BLQ): The Bologna Airport is located about 6 kilometers northwest of the city center and serves as the major aviation gateway to Bologna and the surrounding region.

Foreign Flights: From Bologna Airport, direct flights to major European cities and foreign destinations are available. Flights to and from Bologna are operated by Alitalia, Ryanair, Lufthansa, British Airways, and other carriers.

Transportation from the airport to the city center:

The Aerobus service operates from the airport to the city center. It is a convenient and low-cost option that operates on a regular basis.

Taxis are readily available outside the airport. The journey to the city center takes about 15-20 minutes.

Rental Cars: Several car rental companies have counters at the airport if you prefer to drive yourself.

Taking the Train

Bologna Centrale Railway Station: Bologna Centrale is the city's central train station and a major rail hub in Italy.

High-speed trains connect Bologna to major Italian towns like Rome, Florence, Milan, Venice, and Naples. The Frecciarossa and Italo trains are fast and comfortable modes of transportation.

Regional Trains: Bologna has a well-developed regional train network that connects it to smaller towns and cities throughout Emilia-Romagna and nearby regions.

Within the city limits of Bologna:

Bologna features an efficient public transportation system that includes buses and a light rail system called as "Tramvia." Tickets can be purchased at tobacco shops, ticket machines, or onboard the vehicles.

Walking: The historic center of Bologna is small and pedestrian-friendly, making it easy to explore on foot.

Taking the Bus

Long-Distance Buses: Long-distance bus services connect Bologna to other Italian municipalities as well as international destinations.

FlixBus: FlixBus is a well-known long-distance bus company that offers low-cost connections to cities throughout Italy and neighboring countries.

Within the city limits of Bologna:

Bologna has a large network of urban buses that cover the city and its surrounds, providing an additional form of transportation.

Visiting Local Attractions

Bologna's strategic location in Emilia-Romagna makes it a good base for day trips to nearby destinations.

By Train: Several significant attractions, including Florence, Venice, and Ravenna, are easily accessible by train from Bologna.

By Bus: Day tours and shuttle services are available to key destinations like as Modena (famous for balsamic vinegar), Parma (famous for Parmigiano Reggiano cheese), and the Ferrari Museum in Maranello.

Traveling to and around Bologna is simple because to the city's strong transportation connections, whether by flight, train, or bus. Once in the city, there are several possibilities to learn about the city's rich cultural history as well as nearby riches in Emilia-Romagna.

2.5. Getting Around Bologna (Public Transportation, Walking, Biking, Renting a Car)

Exploring Bologna is a delight, and there are numerous practical transit options to let you discover its historic streets and distinct neighborhoods. Here's a complete guide to getting about Bologna:

Transportation by Public

Buses: In Bologna, TPER (Trasporto Passeggeri Emilia-Romagna) runs an efficient and well-developed bus network. The entire city, including the historic core and the suburbs, is served by buses. They operate from early morning until late at night, making it easy to get around.

Tickets can be purchased from authorized resellers, tabaccherie (tobacco shops), or automatic ticket machines at bus stops. There are numerous ticket kinds available, including single rides, daily passes, and weekly passes.

Tramvia: Bologna also has a light rail system called "Tramvia" that connects many important locations throughout the city. Tram lines are a practical and environmentally friendly means of transportation.

Walking

Bologna's medieval core is a pedestrian's paradise. Because the city is compact and easily navigable on foot, walking is one of the best ways to discover its gorgeous streets, arcades, and secret corners.

Piazza Maggiore: Begin your journey at the city's central plaza, Piazza Maggiore, and work your way through the surrounding streets to visit historical landmarks, museums, and lively piazzas.

Bologna is famous for its porticos, which stretch for approximately 38 kilometers. These covered arcades give rain and sun protection, making walking in all weather situations comfortable.

Biking

Cycling is a major mode of transportation in Bologna, and it is popular with both locals and visitors.

Bike Sharing: Bologna offers a bike-sharing system called "BiciBo," which allows you to rent bicycles from various stations placed across the city. To begin exploring on two wheels, simply register online or at the bike stations.

Bike Rentals: There are several bike rental shops in Bologna where you can rent bicycles for a day or longer and explore the city and its surrounds at your leisure.

Bologna has designated bicycle paths and lanes that make riding around the city both safe and enjoyable.

Rental of a vehicle

While the historic center of Bologna is mostly pedestrian-only, renting a car can be useful if you want to explore the surrounding countryside and local attractions.

Car rental companies in Bologna include both huge international names and local operations.

Hertz: Hertz is one of the world's largest and best-known car rental companies, with a branch at Bologna Guglielmo Marconi Airport and several other locations throughout the city.

Avis is another reputable car rental firm with locations at Bologna Airport and throughout the city center, making it easy for visitors to rent a car upon arrival.

Europcar: Europcar is a well-known car rental company with a wide range of vehicles and facilities in Bologna, including the airport and main train station.

Sixt: Sixt is a well-known car rental company with numerous outlets in Bologna, offering a diverse range of automobiles to fulfill a variety of travel needs.

Budget: Budget has a presence at Bologna Airport as well as other significant locations throughout the city and provides low-cost accommodations.

Maggiore: Maggiore is a local car rental brand with a strong presence in Bologna, offering a wide range of vehicles for both leisure and business travelers to rent.

Winrent: Although Winrent is a newer player in the car rental industry, it has quickly gained popularity in Bologna thanks to its affordable prices and good service.

Locauto Rent is another car rental option, with facilities at Bologna Airport and other convenient locations.

When renting a car in Bologna, you must have a valid driver's license and a credit card for the rental transaction. Additionally, familiarize yourself with local traffic rules and parking limits to guarantee a smooth and comfortable driving experience across the city and beyond.

Check rates, vehicle selections, and rental terms from different car rental providers to get the best price for your holiday goals and budget.

Parking: If you rent a car, look for garages or parking spots outside the ZTL (Zona a Traffico Limitato) zone, as driving within the restricted zone is only permitted for residents and licensed vehicles.

The historic heart of Bologna is a ZTL (Prohibited Traffic Zone), which implies that traffic is prohibited. Non-resident automobiles are typically not permitted within the ZTL, save at particular periods and regions. Parking your car outside the ZTL and taking public transportation or walking to the central area is preferable.

Signs indicating "Limited Traffic Zones" can be found in numerous neighborhoods throughout Bologna. Pay attention to these indicators to avoid fines and penalties.

Traffic and ZTL Cameras: There are traffic and ZTL cameras all across Bologna. Even if you are a tourist, offenses may result in fines being issued to the vehicle's owner.

Bologna's efficient public transportation system, pedestrian-friendly streets, bike-sharing choices, and car rental businesses provide a variety of transportation options. Whether you like to walk, cycle, or take public transportation, you can easily explore this fascinating city and make the most of your tour.

Accommodation

3.1. Overview of Various Neighborhoods

Bologna has a wide variety of neighborhoods, each with its own distinct personality and charm. Whether you want to stay in the historic center or in a quieter residential region, Bologna has a neighborhood to suit every traveler's needs. Here's a rundown of some of the more well-known neighborhoods:

Centro Storico (Historical Center)

The Historic Center is the beating heart of Bologna, including the majority of the city's notable sites, gorgeous architecture, and bustling atmosphere. The tiny lanes, stately palaces, and famous red-brick medieval towers identify the neighborhood.

Advantages:

Attractions: Staying in the Historic Center puts you within walking distance of major attractions such as Piazza Maggiore, the Two Towers, the Basilica di San Petronio, and Archiginnasio.

The area comes alive at night with numerous pubs, restaurants, and entertainment options.

Immerse yourself in true Bolognese culture by being surrounded by residents and their daily routines.

Tourist Crowds: Because it is the most well-known place, it can become busy, especially during high tourist seasons.

Limited Parking: If you're traveling by car, finding parking in the city center can be difficult.

St. Stefano

The Basilica di Santo Stefano, a complex of seven churches, and the magnificent Piazza Santo Stefano are all located in the Santo Stefano district, which is noted for its medieval elegance.

Advantages:

Experience the medieval landscape with its narrow streets and old buildings.

Quiet and relaxing: Compared to the hectic city center, Santo Stefano provides a more tranquil setting.

Local stores and Cafes: Explore the neighborhood's artisan stores, boutique cafes, and classic trattorias.

Considerations:

Less Touristy: While some may like the peace and quiet, this neighborhood has less tourist-oriented attractions.

Via Zamboni (University District)

The University District, centered on Via Zamboni, is alive and well, thanks to the presence of the University of Bologna, one of the world's oldest universities.

Advantages:

Enjoy the dynamic atmosphere with students, academics, and cultural activities.

Budget-Friendly: You may discover more economical lodging options, particularly in hostels and student houses.

Cafes and Bookstores: Visit unusual cafes, bookstores, and trendy hangouts.

Considerations:

Noise Levels: Due to the area's youth, it may get vibrant and raucous, especially on weekends.

Bolognina

Bolognina, a residential district just beyond the historic center, has a combination of ancient and new buildings.

Advantages:

Local Flavor: Discover a less-touristy side of the city.

Affordability: Accommodation in Bolognina may be less expensive than in the city center.

Public Transportation: The city center is easily accessible by public transportation.

Considerations:

Distance from the City Center: While public transportation is available, it may take a little longer to get to the main attractions.

The town of San Donato

San Donato is a peaceful neighborhood northeast of the city center known for its parks and green spaces.

Advantages:

Quiet Retreat: Relax and unwind away from the hustle and bustle of the city core.

San Donato has various parks and gardens that provide a calm environment.

Local Restaurants: Explore charming trattorias and local eateries.

Considerations:

Distance from Major Attractions: Because it is further from the major tourist attractions, you may need to take public transportation to get to the city center.

From the historical charm of the city center to the calm recesses of San Donato, each district of Bologna provides a distinct experience. When deciding on the neighborhood that best matches your stay in this enchanting Italian city, consider your preferences for ambiance, proximity to attractions, and price.

3.2. Hotels

Bologna has a wide assortment of hotels, from luxury to budget-friendly options. Here are some wonderful hotels in various neighborhoods to consider for your stay:

The Historic Center

Grand Hotel Majestic "già Baglioni" (5-star): This magnificent hotel is located near Piazza Maggiore in a historic palace. Elegant rooms, a rooftop deck with panoramic views, and a gourmet restaurant are available.

Art Hotel Commercianti (4-star): This boutique hotel is just steps away from the Two Towers and boasts nicely designed rooms with a mix of modern and antique furniture.

Hotel Corona d'Oro (4-star): This hotel combines historical elegance with modern conveniences and is housed in a renovated medieval building. It offers a lovely rooftop deck and is strategically located.

Hotel Cavour (4-star): This hotel offers nice accommodations and a wonderful garden balcony near the Basilica di Santo Stefano. It is a short distance from the city center.

Hotel Metropolitan (3-star): Located on a quiet street near Piazza Santo Stefano, this modern hotel has contemporary rooms and a nice bar area.

Via Zamboni (University District)

The quaint Albergo delle Drapperie (3-star) is adjacent to Via Zamboni and Piazza Maggiore. It creates comfortable interiors with a rustic appeal.

Hotel University (3-star): This hotel is conveniently located near the University of Bologna and offers nice rooms as well as easy access to cultural landmarks.

Hotel Mercure Bologna Centro (4-star): This modern hotel in the Bolognina neighborhood features well-appointed rooms and a fitness center. The city center is conveniently accessible via public transportation.

Hotel Michelino Bologna Fiera (3-star): Located near the Bologna Fiere exhibition area, this hotel offers affordable lodging with easy access to public transportation.

Hotel Holiday (4-star): Located in the San Donato district, this hotel offers modern rooms, an on-site restaurant, and a fitness facility.

Savoia Hotel Regency (4-star): Surrounded by vegetation, this exquisite hotel provides a tranquil haven with a large outdoor pool and spacious suites.

Remember to book your accommodations ahead of time, especially during peak tourist seasons. The hotels listed above cater to a variety of budgets and preferences, allowing you to discover the ideal location to make the most of your time in picturesque Bologna.

3.3. B&B (Bed and Breakfast)

A stay at a Bologna Bed and Breakfast (B&B) provides a more intimate and personalized experience. Here is a list of several great B&B options in various neighborhoods to consider for your stay:

The Historic Center

B&B Casa Bologna: Located in the heart of the old center, this quaint B&B offers comfortable rooms with a combination of modern and classic design. The warm welcome and helpful advice for seeing the city are provided by the pleasant hosts.

B&B Cavour: This quaint B&B near Piazza Maggiore has attractively designed rooms and a shared kitchenette. The central location and pleasant staff are popular among guests.

Santo Stefano Bed and Breakfast: This B&B is located in the Santo Stefano district and offers magnificent rooms as well as a serene garden balcony. The location is ideal for walking around historic sites.

B&B Milazzo: This B&B offers pleasant rooms and a delicious Italian breakfast near the Basilica of Santo Stefano. The hosts are well-known for their friendliness and local recommendations.

B&B Via del Carro: Located near Via Zamboni and the university, this B&B offers light and cheerful rooms with a communal lounge space. Guests appreciate the friendly atmosphere and easy location.

B&B Dolce Risveglio: This B&B near the campus offers elegant accommodations and a delicious breakfast. The welcoming hosts go above and above to make guests feel at ease.

B&B Design: This modern B&B in the Bolognina neighborhood offers elegant rooms and a shared sitting space. It has good public transportation connections, making it easy to get to the city center.

B&B Chez Moi: This warm and inviting B&B in Bolognina offers comfortable accommodations and a welcome ambiance. The hosts are well-known for their friendliness and assistance.

B&B Pitstop: This B&B offers pleasant rooms and a garden deck in the calm San Donato neighborhood. Guests like the peaceful settings and easy access to green spaces.

B&B Villa Marsa: Located in San Donato Park, this B&B offers a tranquil environment, comfortable accommodations, and a delicious breakfast. The hosts ensure a relaxing stay.

Staying at a B&B in Bologna allows you to see the city through the eyes of residents while also receiving personalized treatment. The options offered offer a variety of amenities and settings to fit a variety of interests, making your visit to Bologna really unique.

3.4. Vacation Rentals and Apartments

Renting an apartment or holiday rental is a good choice if you desire a more independent and home-like experience during your time in Bologna. Here is a list of several decent flats and holiday rentals to consider in various areas:

The Historic Center

Residenza Ariosto: This magnificent apartment in the historic center offers attractive and spacious accommodations with modern facilities.

Santo Stefano Loft: Located near Piazza Santo Stefano, this quaint loft apartment with a fully equipped kitchen offers a comfortable and romantic setting.

Casa Zamboni 15: This modern and bright apartment is close to Via Zamboni and the university, providing a comfortable accommodation with a city view.

Cozy Loft University: A charming loft apartment with a modern style, conveniently located near the university district and busy cafes.

Modern Bolognina Apartment: This modern Bolognina apartment has all of the conveniences of home, as well as easy access to public transportation and neighboring facilities.

Bolognina Garden Retreat: Unwind after a day of exploration by staying in this beautiful apartment with a private garden.

San Donato Peaceful Home: This apartment in the serene San Donato district offers a peaceful getaway with a fully equipped kitchen and excellent views.

Green Oasis Apartment: This charming apartment near San Donato Park offers a quiet atmosphere surrounded by nature.

Areas Surrounding

Villa in the Bolognese Hills: For a more rural experience, consider renting a villa in the magnificent Bolognese hills, which provide a peaceful respite from the city.

Farmhouse Getaway: Experience the rustic appeal of the countryside by staying in a classic Italian farmhouse.

Renting an apartment or vacation rental in Bologna gives you your own place and allows you to see the city like a local. The options offered provide a variety of features and settings, allowing you to enjoy your Bologna journey at your own speed.

3.5 Hostels and Low-Cost Accommodations

Bologna has a selection of hostels and cheap hotels that provide comfort and convenience for budget-conscious guests. Here is a selection of good hostels and low-cost options to consider for your stay:

Hostels

We_Bologna Hostel: This trendy and environmentally friendly hostel is close to the train station and the historic center. It has a lively environment, comfortable dorms and private rooms, a shared kitchen, and open areas.

Dopa Hostel: Dopa Hostel is located in the centre of the city and offers modern and cozy dorms with lockers. It's a short walk to main sights and busy nightlife.

Accommodations at a Low Cost

Hotel San Giorgio: This low-cost hotel is close to the Bologna Centrale Railway Station. It provides modest and clean rooms with all of the necessities for a comfortable stay.

Albergo Panorama: Albergo Panorama is a budget-friendly hotel with a central position that offers pleasant rooms and a warm ambiance.

Bed and breakfasts

B&B Hope: Located in the historic district, B&B Hope offers affordable rooms with a shared kitchen and a welcoming atmosphere.

Le Stanze del Carro: This guesthouse in the University District offers basic and affordable rooms close to famous landmarks.

Apartments in a Hostel

Student's Hostel Bologna: This hostel provides both dormitory beds and private apartments, making it ideal for groups or travelers who prefer a more private environment. It is near the University of Bologna and other amenities.

Bologna Center Town: A hostel-style apartment with multiple rooms and shared facilities that provides a cost-effective option for both groups and solo travelers.

These Bologna hostels and budget-friendly accommodations are an excellent choice for travelers looking to save money on lodging while still having a comfortable and convenient stay.

Attractions and Sightseeing

4.1. Piazza Maggiore and Palazzo Comunale

Welcome to Piazza Maggiore, the beating heart of Bologna! This magnificent square, surrounded by historical landmarks and lively energy, is a must-visit draw during your time in the city. Let's journey into the enchanting world of Piazza Maggiore and its centerpiece, Palazzo Comunale.

Piazza Maggiore

A Vibrant Gathering Place: Piazza Maggiore is the main square of Bologna, and it has been the city's social and cultural center for ages. The square's vast open space invites both locals and tourists to meet, relax, and soak in the lively ambiance.

Historical Significance: The square goes back to the 13th century and has witnessed numerous historical events. It has been the backdrop for public meetings, celebrations, and even political gatherings, making it a place of great importance for Bologna's character.

Basilica di San Petronio: At the southern end of the square stands the grand Basilica di San Petronio, one of the biggest churches in Europe. Its striking facade and intricate interior showcase a fusion of architectural styles, reflecting the city's rich past.

Palazzo dei Notai and Palazzo d'Accursio: Alongside the Basilica, you'll find the Palazzo dei Notai and Palazzo d'Accursio, two impressive buildings with unique histories. Palazzo dei Notai was the home of the city's notaries, while Palazzo d'Accursio served as the city hall.

Fontana del Nettuno: In the center of Piazza Maggiore stands the majestic Fontana del Nettuno, a captivating pond featuring the mythical sea god Neptune. The fountain is a symbol of Bologna's maritime power and artistic history.

Cafés and Street Performers: As you explore the square, you'll encounter charming cafés lining its edges, offering a perfect spot to enjoy a coffee or aperitivo while watching the vibrant city life. Street performers often add to the lively atmosphere, enchanting tourists with their talents.

Palazzo Comunale (City Hall)

Bologna's Administrative Hub: Palazzo Comunale, also known as Palazzo d'Accursio, has been the seat of

Bologna's government for ages. This historical building shows the city's political and cultural evolution throughout the ages.

Impressive Architecture: The palace displays a harmonious blend of architectural styles, from the medieval façade to Renaissance and Baroque elements added over time. The delicate frescoes and ornate decorations inside the palace offer a glimpse into Bologna's rich artistic history.

The Sala Farnese: Don't miss the magnificent Sala Farnese, an opulent hall adorned with frescoes by famous artists Annibale Carracci and his brother Agostino Carracci. The paintings show historical events and allegorical figures, giving insight into Bologna's storied past.

The Sala Rossa: Another gem within Palazzo Comunale is the Sala Rossa (Red Room), an exquisite room decorated with red damask silk and precious decorations. It's a testament to the palace's grandeur and historical importance.

The Museum of Palazzo Comunale: The palace also houses the Museum of Palazzo Comunale, where you can explore an amazing collection of art, historical artifacts, and documents that offer further insights into the city's past.

Panoramic Views: After immersing yourself in the palace's grand rooms, head up to the Torre dell'Arengo or the Torre Asinelli, the tallest towers in Bologna. From these vantage places, you can enjoy breathtaking panoramic views of the city and its surroundings.

As you stand in awe of the grandeur of Piazza Maggiore and Palazzo Comunale, take a moment to enjoy the rich history and cultural significance of these remarkable landmarks. Embrace the vibrant atmosphere, connect with the locals, and cherish the timeless beauty that Bologna has to offer.

4.2. Basilica di San Petronio

Welcome to the awe-inspiring Basilica di San Petronio, a true gem of Bologna! This majestic church holds a special place in the hearts of Bolognese people and stands as a symbol of the city's historical and religious importance. Let's discover the captivating details of this iconic landmark:

A Grand Religious Monument

Gothic Splendor: The Basilica di San Petronio is an extraordinary example of Italian Gothic building. Its imposing facade displays intricate details, with stunning pink and white marble that glows under the sunlight.

The Unfinished Facade: As you look at the facade, you might notice something intriguing. The church's exterior is unfinished, leaving a mix of raw brick and marble. Legend has it that the building stopped because it was becoming grander than St. Peter's Basilica in Rome, and the Pope intervened to halt its completion.

An Ambitious Project: The building of San Petronio began in 1390 and continued for centuries. Although it was meant to be the largest church in the world, it was never fully completed. Nevertheless, it remains one of the most impressive religious buildings in Italy.

Entering the Basilica

The Main Entrance: Step inside the Basilica through the center portal and be prepared to be mesmerized. The vast interior welcomes you with a feeling of grandeur and reverence.

Spectacular Nave: The interior of San Petronio is astonishingly vast, with a nave that runs over 132 meters (433 feet) in length and soars up to 45 meters (148 feet) in height. The nave is flanked by tall, slender columns that give a sense of verticality.

Intricate Stained Glass Windows: Look up to the magnificent stained glass windows that fill the aisle with a kaleidoscope of colors when the sunlight streams through. The windows show various religious scenes and saints, adding to the ethereal atmosphere

Biblical Art and Statues: Admire the beautiful artwork and statues that adorn the walls and churches. From Renaissance frescoes to sculpted masterpieces, the Basilica houses a rich collection of sacred art that spans several centuries.

The Meridian Line

An Ancient Sundial: Don't miss the interesting Meridian Line on the Basilica's floor. This astronomical marvel is an ancient sundial, created by the astronomer Giovanni Domenico Cassini in the 17th century.

Tracking the Sun: The Meridian Line tracks the movement of the sun throughout the year, casting a spot of light on the floor to show the date. It was used to calculate the exact date of Easter, an important event in the Christian calendar.

Respectful Dress Code

When viewing the Basilica di San Petronio, please keep in mind that it is a place of worship. Modest dress is respected, with shoulders and knees covered as a sign of respect.

As you explore the Basilica di San Petronio, immerse yourself in the beauty of its architecture, the serenity of its interior, and the interesting history it holds. Witness the magnificent craftsmanship and wonder at the Meridian Line, a tribute to the fusion of art, science, and faith in this remarkable place.

4.3. The Two Towers (Asinelli and Garisenda)

Prepare to be enchanted by the famous Two Towers of Bologna, Asinelli and Garisenda! These medieval towers stand tall as a symbol of Bologna's rich past and offer an extraordinary experience for visitors. Let's dig into the fascinating details of these magnificent structures:

The Towering Landmarks

The Asinelli Tower: Asinelli is the taller and more famous of the two towers, rising to a height of approximately 97.2 meters (319 feet). Its impressive height makes it the biggest leaning medieval tower in the world.

The Garisenda Tower: Garisenda, the lower tower, stands at around 47 meters (154 feet) tall. It is easily recognizable by its marked lean, which adds to its unique charm.

Historical Origins: The construction of these towers goes back to the 12th century, a time when Bologna was a thriving medieval city. The noble families of the time made these towers as symbols of power, wealth, and defense.

The Asinelli Tower

Climbing the Asinelli Tower: Today, visitors have the chance to climb the 498 steps of the Asinelli Tower to reach the top. As you ascend, the spiral staircase offers glimpses of the tower's sturdy construction.

Breathtaking Views: The effort of climbing is repaid with breathtaking panoramic views of Bologna and the surrounding countryside. From this vantage point, you can truly enjoy the beauty and layout of the city.

The Stone Forest: At the top, you'll meet the "Stone Forest" – a fascinating display of medieval stone structures that support the tower's wooden platform.

A Symbol of Freedom: During the Middle Ages, these towers were not only symbols of power but also of liberty. They reflected the city's independence from outside rulers.

The Garisenda Tower

An Inclined Wonder: The Garisenda Tower leans significantly, leading it to be closed to visitors for safety reasons. However, its lean is a testament to the engineering problems faced by builders in the Middle Ages.

Historical Lean: The lean of the Garisenda Tower was even more pronounced in the past, but it was partly straightened out over the centuries to prevent it from toppling.

Literary Inspiration: The lean of the Garisenda Tower is described in Dante Alighieri's "Divine Comedy," cementing its place in literary history.

Visiting Tips

Tickets and Hours: To climb the Asinelli Tower, you'll need to buy tickets from the entrance. It's best to check the opening hours in advance, as they can change throughout the year.

Fitness Level: Climbing the Asinelli Tower involves a considerable number of steps, so it's suggested for visitors with a moderate level of fitness.

Restoration and Preservation: Both towers have undergone extensive restoration work over the years to ensure their longevity and safety for tourists.

As you stand in awe of the Two Towers, you'll feel transported back in time to the medieval era, feeling the majesty and ingenuity of Bologna's past. Whether you marvel at the height of Asinelli or the lean of Garisenda, these towers will leave an indelible impact on your journey through this captivating city.

4.4. Archiginnasio of Bologna

Welcome to the remarkable Archiginnasio of Bologna, a treasure trove of history and study! This ancient building holds a special place in the city's heart as the former seat of the University of Bologna, the oldest university in the Western world. Prepare to be captivated by the fascinating details and importance of the Archiginnasio:

Historical Background

A Seat of Learning: The Archiginnasio was built between 1562 and 1563 to house the University of Bologna, which was created in 1088. It served as the main building for the university until the 19th century when the institution moved to its current site.

Architectural Marvel: The building's architecture showcases the grandeur and elegance of the Renaissance era. The stunning facade is adorned with sculptures, coats of arms, and inscriptions that celebrate knowledge and academic success

The Anatomy Theater: One of the highlights of the Archiginnasio is the Anatomical Theater, a wonder of anatomical science. This circular amphitheater, built for anatomy lectures and dissections, is a testimony to Bologna's pioneering role in medical education.

The Anatomy Theater

A Glimpse into Medical Education: The Anatomy Theater was finished in 1637, and it's one of the oldest remaining anatomical theaters in the world. The students would gather in the semicircular tiered seats to watch dissections performed by skilled anatomists.

Elaborate Wooden Structure: The theater's wooden interior is a masterpiece of handiwork, featuring elaborate carvings, decorative elements, and a domed ceiling with allegorical paintings.

The Professor's Chair: At the center of the theater stands the Professor's Chair, an ornate seat where the respected anatomist would conduct the dissections and lectures.

The Aula Magna

The Great Hall: The Aula Magna (Great Hall) is another feature of the Archiginnasio. This majestic room was used for important academic events, graduation ceremonies, and talks.

Famous Portraits: The walls of the Aula Magna are adorned with portraits of illustrious scholars and important figures connected with the University of Bologna. These portraits celebrate the university's intellectual history.

Visiting Tips

Guided Tours: When you visit the Archiginnasio, consider taking a guided tour to fully appreciate the historical importance and intricate details of this magnificent building.

Respectful Attire: As a place of historical and academic importance, please dress modestly when viewing the Archiginnasio as a sign of respect.

Library Hall: While you explore the Archiginnasio, don't miss the Library Hall (Sala di Lettura), which houses a rich collection of rare books and papers.

Preserving History

The Archiginnasio experienced damage during World War II, but extensive restoration work has preserved its splendor for future generations to admire. Today, it houses the Archiginnasio Municipal Library and is a testament to Bologna's enduring dedication to education and knowledge.

As you step into the Archiginnasio, you'll be transported through the annals of time, feeling the profound connection between Bologna's past and its vibrant academic present. This magnificent building stands as a testament to the enduring spirit of knowledge and the quest of learning.

4.5. Santo Stefano Basilica

Step into the lovely Santo Stefano Basilica complex, also known as the Seven Churches of Santo Stefano! This unique and sacred site in Bologna is a captivating blend of history, legend, and spiritual importance. Prepare to be immersed in the amazing details of this remarkable place of worship:

The Seven Churches of Santo Stefano

An Intriguing Complex: The Santo Stefano Basilica is not a single church but a complex of seven linked churches and chapels, each with its own distinct character and history.

The Church of the Holy Sepulchre: One of the oldest and most important churches in the complex, the Church of the Holy Sepulchre, features a central dome and stunning Romanesque architecture.

The Church of the Saints Vitale and Agricola: This church is dedicated to Saints Vitale and Agricola and boasts a beautiful cloister decorated with elegant columns and arches.

The Church of the Saints Sepolcro and Stefano: Connected to the previous church, this chapel's design shows a blend of Romanesque and Gothic elements.

The Church of the Crucifix: As the name suggests, this church houses a revered crucifix and is known for its charming simplicity.

The Church of San Giovanni in Fonte: This small church is famous for its unique octagonal shape and is said to have been built over a spring where Saint Petronius baptized early Christian converts.

The Church of the Trinity: This church was dedicated to the Holy Trinity and boasts amazing frescoes and a beautiful altar.

The Church of the Saints Vitale and Agricola (the New Church): Different from the previous church of the same name, this one was built later and features a lovely portico.

Historical Significance

A Place of Pilgrimage: Santo Stefano Basilica has been a pilgrimage site for centuries, drawing both locals and tourists seeking spiritual solace.

The Legend of St. Petronius: Legend has it that Saint Petronius, the patron saint of Bologna, ordered the building of the complex after having a vision of the Holy Sepulchre in Jerusalem. The Seven Churches were built to replicate the holy places he saw in his vision.

The Palms of Saint Peter: Inside the complex, you'll find an ancient courtyard with palm trees, a reference to Saint Peter, who is said to have placed them himself.

Exploring the Complex

Peaceful Courtyards: As you wander through the basilica's different courtyards and cloisters, you'll experience a profound feeling of tranquility and spirituality.

Chapels and Altars: Each church within the complex houses precious altars, intricate frescoes, and religious artifacts, giving a glimpse into the rich religious history of Bologna.

Visiting Tips: The Basilica complex is an important religious site, so please remember to dress modestly as a sign of respect when visiting.

Preserving Sacred Heritage

The Santo Stefano Basilica complex has undergone careful preservation and restoration efforts to preserve its historical and architectural heritage. The site stands as a testament to Bologna's deep-rooted religious traditions and its dedication to preserving sacred landmarks for future generations.

As you step into the Santo Stefano Basilica complex, you'll start on a journey through centuries of devotion and devotion to faith. The Seven Churches of Santo Stefano offer a profound and soul-stirring experience, where history, legend, and spirituality meet.

4.6. Museo Civico Archeologico

Welcome to the fascinating Museo Civico Archeologico, where history comes to life! This archaeological museum in Bologna houses a wealth of ancient artifacts and treasures that offer an interesting glimpse into the region's rich past. Let's start on a journey through the museum's intriguing exhibits:

Discovering Ancient Etruria and Beyond

A Journey Back in Time: The Museo Civico Archeologico takes you on a journey through time, starting from the prehistoric age to the Roman and Etruscan civilizations.

The Etruscan Collection: The museum's Etruscan collection is particularly noteworthy, featuring rare artifacts from the ancient Etruscan culture that once thrived in the area.

Roman Artifacts: Marvel at an array of Roman sculptures, inscriptions, and everyday items that provide valuable insights into the daily life and cultural practices of the Romans.

The Famous Etruscan Bronze Liver of Piacenza

An Archaeological Marvel: The museum proudly displays the famous Etruscan Bronze Liver of Piacenza, a unique artifact going back to the 2nd century BC.

Divination and Rituals: This detailed bronze model of a sheep's liver was used for divination practices by Etruscan priests. Its engravings and inscriptions were thought to reveal insights into the gods' will.

Symbol of Etruscan Knowledge: The Liver of Piacenza is regarded as one of the most important Etruscan artifacts ever found and is a testament to the advanced knowledge and beliefs of this ancient culture.

Elegant Mosaics and Frescoes

Roman Mosaics: Admire the exquisite Roman mosaics on display, showing intricate designs and patterns that once adorned the floors of luxurious villas and public buildings.

Frescoes from Pompeii: Be captivated by the vibrant frescoes that were carefully excavated from the ruins of Pompeii, showing scenes of everyday life, mythological tales, and stunning landscapes.

The Egyptian Collection

Egyptian Artifacts: The museum also boasts an amazing collection of Egyptian artifacts, including statues, funerary objects, and hieroglyphic inscriptions.

The Mummy Case: One of the highlights of the Egyptian collection is a beautifully decorated mummy case that shows the ancient Egyptian beliefs about the afterlife.

Exploring the Museum

Interactive Displays: The museum features interactive displays and multimedia presentations that enhance the visitor's experience, giving deeper insights into the artifacts and their historical context.

Educational Programs: The Museo Civico Archeologico regularly hosts educational programs, workshops, and guided tours to interest visitors of all ages with the wonders of archaeology.

Visiting Tips: Plan to spend at least a few hours exploring the museum to fully enjoy its vast collection of ancient treasures.

Preserving Ancient Heritage

The Museo Civico Archeologico is committed to preserving and showcasing the invaluable archaeological history of Bologna and its surrounding regions. The artifacts on display are carefully curated, allowing visitors to connect with the past in a meaningful and profound way.

As you wander through the Museo Civico Archeologico, you'll start on a captivating trip through time, immersing yourself in the splendor and mysteries of ancient civilizations. The museum's collection stands as a testament to the enduring allure of archaeology and the timeless human drive to uncover our past.

4.7. Porticoes of Bologna

Step into a world of architectural marvels with the famous Porticoes of Bologna, a defining feature of the city's scenery! These covered walkways have been an important part of Bologna's urban fabric for centuries, offering both practicality and beauty. Let's study the fascinating details of these iconic structures:

A City of Porticoes

Unique Urban Feature: Bologna is famous for its extensive network of porticoes, with over 38 kilometers (about 24 miles) of covered walkways that crisscross the city. This makes it the place with the longest porticoes in the world.

Historical Roots: The tradition of building porticoes in Bologna goes back to ancient times, but they became more prevalent during the medieval and Renaissance periods. They were built to meet practical needs while also showcasing the city's wealth and architectural prowess.

Practical uses: The porticoes served several practical uses. They gave shelter from the weather, protecting pedestrians from rain and snow. They also provided shaded areas during hot summers, making walking more comfortable. Additionally, the porticoes acted as extensions of residential and commercial spaces, expanding the usable area of buildings.

The Iconic Three-and-Four Series

The Three Series: Bologna's porticoes are classified into three main series based on their historical growth. The "Three Series" includes porticoes built during the medieval and Renaissance times, featuring stunning arches and elegant columns.

The Four Series: The "Four Series" comprises porticoes from the 19th and 20th centuries, distinguished by simpler designs and straighter lines. Despite their more modest appearance, they maintain the functional and architectural essence of the portico tradition.

Historical Landmarks

Portico di San Luca: Among the most famous is the Portico di San Luca, a monumental covered walkway that runs for over 3.5 kilometers (about 2.2 miles) and leads to the Basilica di San Luca atop Colle della Guardia. This historic portico is a treasured symbol of Bologna and offers breathtaking views of the city below.

Portico del Pavaglione: The Portico del Pavaglione, found along Via dell'Indipendenza, is another iconic landmark. It features a double row of arches, creating a striking visual effect that adds to the grandeur of the city's main street.

Modern and Vibrant Spaces

A Living Urban Canvas: Bologna's porticoes are not just relics of the past; they continue to be vital to the city's daily life. Today, many of the arches are filled with shops, boutiques, cafes, and restaurants, providing a vibrant and dynamic urban experience.

The "Longest Museum in the World": The porticoes have earned the nickname "The Longest Museum in the World" due to the numerous art works and exhibitions that adorn the arches, transforming the city's walkways into a living art gallery.

Appreciating the Porticoes

Strolling Through History: As you stroll along Bologna's porticoes, take the time to enjoy the architectural nuances, the play of light and shadow, and the seamless integration of ancient history with modern life.

A Local Tradition: For locals, walking through the porticoes is not just a means of getting around the city; it's a cherished tradition that connects them to their heritage and gives a sense of belonging.

Preserving a Cultural Legacy

The Porticoes of Bologna are a UNESCO World Heritage Site, recognized for their exceptional cultural and historical importance. The city takes great pride in keeping these architectural treasures for future generations to enjoy.

As you start on a journey through the Porticoes of Bologna, you'll immerse yourself in the rich tapestry of history, architecture, and vibrant city life. These covered walkways are not only a testament to Bologna's past but also a live testament to the enduring spirit of this remarkable city.

4.8. Giardini Margherita

Welcome to Giardini Margherita, Bologna's beloved urban oasis! This sprawling park, nestled in the heart of the city, offers a delightful escape from the hustle and bustle, inviting both locals and tourists to unwind and connect with nature. Let's discover the captivating details of Giardini Margherita:

Historical Roots

Royal Origins: Giardini Margherita was formed in the late 19th century, designed by architect Ernesto Basile under the direction of King Umberto I and Queen Margherita of Italy. It was named in honor of Queen Margherita, known for her love of the arts and nature.

A Gift to the City: The park was a gift from the royal family to the citizens of Bologna, a gesture that was deeply appreciated by the local community.

Lush Greenery and Scenic Beauty

Expansive Green Spaces: The park spans over 26 hectares (about 64 acres) and features an enchanting environment of sprawling lawns, leafy trees, and bright flowerbeds. It's the perfect place for relaxed strolls or picnics with family and friends.

Lake and Fountains: A beautiful lake adds to the park's charm, providing a tranquil setting for relaxing by the water's edge. Nearby waterfalls add a soothing soundtrack to the park's ambiance.

Botanical Diversity: Giardini Margherita is home to a wide variety of plants and trees, making it an ideal spot for nature lovers and photographers.

Recreation and Outdoor Activities

Playgrounds for All Ages: The park boasts several well-equipped playgrounds that cater to children of all ages, ensuring that the little ones have an amazing time.

Sports Facilities: Giardini Margherita offers various sports facilities, including tennis courts, soccer fields, and basketball courts. It's a hub for outdoor sports and pastimes.

Boating on the Lake: During the warm months, tourists can rent rowboats and paddleboats to enjoy a leisurely ride on the serene lake.

Jogging and Cycling: The park's paved paths are perfect for jogging and cycling, allowing fitness enthusiasts to enjoy their workouts amidst a lush green background.

Cultural and Social Hub

Outdoor Events: Throughout the year, Giardini Margherita hosts a myriad of cultural events, concerts, and fairs. From live music performances to open-air theater shows, there's always something exciting going in the park.

Relaxing Cafés: Several charming cafés and kiosks are spread throughout the park, providing a lovely spot to enjoy a coffee or a refreshing drink.

Family-Friendly Atmosphere

Families and Friends: Giardini Margherita is a meeting place for families and friends, where generations come together to bond and make cherished memories.

Pet-Friendly: The park welcomes well-behaved pets, making it a favorite location for dog owners who can enjoy leisurely walks with their furry companions.

Preserving Natural Beauty

Giardini Margherita is carefully kept and cherished by the city of Bologna as a precious natural and cultural heritage. It continues to be a beloved destination for both locals wanting relaxation and visitors looking to experience the authentic spirit of Bologna.

As you step into Giardini Margherita, you'll be embraced by the serene beauty and vibrant atmosphere that make it a cherished part of Bologna's character. Whether you seek tranquility, recreation, or cultural experiences, this park offers a harmonious mix of nature and urban life.

4.9. Museo d'Arte Moderna di Bologna (MAMbo)

Welcome to the Museo d'Arte Moderna di Bologna, affectionately known as MAMbo, where modern art takes center stage! This dynamic museum displays an impressive collection of modern and contemporary artworks, providing an enriching experience for art enthusiasts and curious visitors alike. Let's dig into the captivating details of MAMbo:

A Hub for Contemporary Art

A Modern Marvel: Housed in a former bakery in the heart of Bologna, MAMbo is itself a gem of modern architecture. The industrial-chic design serves as a fitting backdrop for the museum's modern art exhibitions.

Expansive Exhibition Spaces: MAMbo spans multiple floors, having over 3,000 square meters (about 32,000 square feet) of exhibition space. Its galleries are thoughtfully curated to present a diverse range of modern artworks and artistic expressions.

The Permanent Collection

Italian Art of the 20th and 21st Centuries: The museum's permanent collection shows an extensive selection of artworks by Italian artists from the 20th century to the present day. You'll meet paintings, sculptures, photographs, videos, and installations that reflect the evolution of art in Italy and beyond.

A Journey Through Time: As you explore the permanent collection, you'll experience the progression of artistic styles and movements, from early 20th-century avant-garde works to post-war art and contemporary experiments.

Rotating Exhibitions

Dynamic and Evolving: MAMbo is known for its rotating shows that feature both established and emerging artists. These temporary shows allow visitors to see fresh views and cutting-edge artistic expressions.

International Collaboration: The museum partners with art institutions from around the world, bringing exciting international artworks to Bologna's vibrant art scene.

Multimedia Installations and Interactive Art

Engaging Experiences: MAMbo embraces multimedia art forms, showing interactive installations, video art, and digital experiences that blur the boundaries between the viewer and the artwork.

Contemplation and Interaction: Prepare to be immersed in thought-provoking artworks that challenge perceptions, evoke emotions, and urge active engagement.

Events and Educational Programs

Art Talks and Workshops: MAMbo regularly hosts art talks, workshops, and guided tours that provide a better understanding of contemporary art and its cultural context. These events cater to visitors of all ages, making art appreciation available to everyone.

Cultural Gatherings: The museum is a hub for cultural gatherings and social events, creating a sense of community among art lovers and creative minds.

Preserving Contemporary Art Heritage

MAMbo plays a vital role in preserving and promoting Italy's contemporary art history, bridging the gap between past artistic forms and the avant-garde visions of the present.

As you step into MAMbo, you'll start on a journey through the ever-evolving landscape of contemporary art, encountering diverse views and innovative expressions. Whether you're a seasoned art connoisseur or a curious traveler, MAMbo offers an immersive and enriching experience that celebrates the creative spirit of our time.

4.10. Bologna Botanical Garden

Welcome to the Bologna Botanical Garden, a peaceful oasis of biodiversity and natural beauty! Nestled within the historic heart of Bologna, this enchanting garden is a haven for plant lovers, researchers, and curious visitors wanting a serene escape. Let's start on a captivating journey through the Bologna Botanical Garden:

Historical Roots

A Living Legacy: Established in 1568, the Bologna Botanical Garden is one of the oldest university botanical gardens in the world. Its creation was started by Ulisse Aldrovandi, a famous naturalist and professor, making it an integral part of Bologna's academic heritage.

Botanical Research: Since its inception, the garden has served as an important center for botanical research, education, and conservation. Its vast collection of plant species reflects a live archive of biodiversity.

A Living Plant Museum

Floral Diversity: The garden spans over 2.2 hectares (about 5.4 acres) and boasts an astounding array of plant species from different corners of the world. From vibrant flowers to towering trees, each corner of the garden offers a new find.

Greenhouses: Wander through the garden's greenhouses, each carefully managed to recreate specific ecosystems. Step into lush tropical environments, arid desert landscapes, and temperate climates—all within the confines of the yard.

Medicinal and Culinary Plants: Explore sections dedicated to medicinal and culinary plants, where you'll meet a fascinating array of herbs and plants with historical significance.

A Feast for the Senses

Sensory Gardens: Engage your senses in the specialized sensory gardens, where you can touch, smell, and hear the wonders of nature. These spaces are thoughtfully built to provide a multisensory experience.

The Garden of Fragrances: In this delightful corner, find a captivating symphony of smells emanating from fragrant flowers and aromatic plants.

Educational and Research Hub

Botanical Studies: The Bologna Botanical Garden remains an active center for botanical study and education. Students, researchers, and plant enthusiasts come here to deepen their knowledge of plant life and ecological processes.

Conservation Efforts: The garden plays a vital role in preserving endangered plant species and promoting biodiversity conservation. Its efforts add to global efforts to safeguard our planet's natural heritage.

Visiting Tips

Guided Tours: Consider taking a guided tour to fully appreciate the garden's historical importance and the fascinating stories behind its diverse plant life.

Relaxation and reflection: The Bologna Botanical Garden is an idyllic spot for relaxation and reflection. Find a peaceful bench amidst the greenery and immerse yourself in the beauty of nature.

Preserving Nature's Wonders

The Bologna Botanical Garden is more than just a garden; it's a testament to the enduring relationship between people and the natural world, showcasing the beauty and complexity of Earth's biodiversity.

As you step into the Bologna Botanical Garden, you'll be enchanted by the splendor of nature and the rich history that surrounds this living gem. Whether you're a nature enthusiast, a curious traveler, or an aspiring botanist, the garden offers an immersive experience that celebrates the wonders of plant life.

Bologna's Neighborhoods

5.1 Historic Center

Welcome to the heart of Bologna, the enchanting Historic Center, where history, culture, and lively energy meet! As you stroll through its ancient streets and piazzas, you'll be transported back in time while experiencing the vibrant atmosphere of modern Bologna. Let's discover the captivating details of the Historic Center:

Piazza Maggiore

The Central Square: Piazza Maggiore is the beating heart of the Historic Center, a bustling square ringed by historic buildings, cafes, and shops. The grand Basilica di San Petronio dominates the square, showing a stunning blend of Gothic and Renaissance architecture.

Fountain of Neptune: At the center of Piazza Maggiore stands the Fountain of Neptune, a famous Bolognese symbol. This impressive bronze statue of Neptune, the Roman god of the sea, adds to the square's charm and appeal.

Two Towers - Asinelli and Garisenda

Medieval Landmarks: The Asinelli and Garisenda Towers are iconic symbols of Bologna's medieval history. The Asinelli Tower stands tall at about 97 meters (318 feet), giving panoramic views of the city from its top. The shorter Garisenda Tower leans slightly, evoking interest and wonder.

Historical Streets and Porticoes

Porticoed Streets: Wander through the narrow streets of the Historic Center, many of which are adorned with elegant porticoes, giving shelter from the elements and adding a touch of architectural splendor.

Via dell'Indipendenza: This lively boulevard connects Piazza Maggiore to Bologna's train station, and it's lined with shops, boutiques, cafes, and restaurants, making it a favorite spot for both locals and tourists.

Palaces and Squares

Palazzo d'Accursio: This magnificent palace faces Piazza Maggiore and was once the seat of Bologna's government. Today, it houses the City Hall and the Civic Art Collection, showcasing important artworks from Bologna's past.

Palazzo del Podestà: Adjacent to Palazzo d'Accursio, this medieval house boasts a beautiful facade adorned with statues and Gothic decorations.

Piazza Santo Stefano: This charming square is home to the Basilica of Santo Stefano, a collection of seven churches and chapels. The square exudes a tranquil ambiance, making it a perfect spot to rest and absorb the city's past.

Cultural and Culinary Delights

Archiginnasio: Delve into the city's academic past by visiting the Archiginnasio, once the seat of Bologna's university. Marvel at the splendid Anatomical Theater and the impressive library hall.

Traditional Cuisine: The Historic Center is brimming with traditional osterias and trattorias, welcoming you to savor Bologna's renowned culinary delights, such as tortellini, tagliatelle al ragù (Bolognese sauce), and mortadella.

Preserving the Past

UNESCO World Heritage: The Historic Center of Bologna is a UNESCO World Heritage Site, recognized for its well-preserved medieval and Renaissance architecture, as well as its cultural importance.

Lively and Contemporary: While steeped in history, the Historic Center remains an energetic and dynamic part of Bologna's modern life, with a lively student population, bustling markets, and an array of cultural events.

As you explore the Historic Center of Bologna, you'll find yourself immersed in the captivating blend of ancient customs and modern vitality. The majestic palaces, intricate porticoes, and lively squares create a unique ambiance that begs you to savor every moment in this timeless city center.

5.2 University District

Welcome to the vibrant University District of Bologna, where centuries of academic success and youthful energy intertwine! This lively neighborhood is home to one of the oldest colleges in the world, and it exudes a dynamic atmosphere that celebrates learning, creativity, and cultural diversity. Let's discover the captivating details of the University District:

University of Bologna

A Prestigious Legacy: Founded in 1088, the University of Bologna is the oldest university in continuous operation in Europe. Its historic buildings and libraries have witnessed the footsteps of famous scholars and intellectuals throughout the ages.

Alma Mater Studiorum: The university's official Latin name, Alma Mater Studiorum, translates to "Nourishing Mother of Studies," showing its commitment to education and the pursuit of knowledge.

Via Zamboni

Academic Heart: Via Zamboni is the main artery of the University District, lined with colleges, libraries, and student hangouts. This vibrant street pulses with the energy of young minds, making it an ideal place to watch the spirit of university life.

Street of Music: Via Zamboni is often referred to as the "Street of Music" because of the many street artists and musicians who add their tunes to the lively ambiance.

Student Life and Culture

The Spirit of Erasmus: Bologna's University District is known for its foreign community of students. The city kindly welcomes Erasmus students and scholars from around the world, fostering a diverse and inclusive cultural exchange.

Aperitivo Traditions: Experience the local aperitivo culture, where students and locals gather in bars and cafes to socialize over drinks and appetizers, creating a convivial and welcoming environment.

Piazza Verdi

Cultural Hub: Piazza Verdi is a popular meeting spot and gathering place for students. It's named after the famous Italian composer, Giuseppe Verdi, and often hosts concerts, performances, and cultural events.

Teatro Comunale: The historic Teatro Comunale, located on Piazza Verdi, is a renowned opera house that has held illustrious performers and opera premieres.

Cultural Institutions

Cineteca di Bologna: Film enthusiasts will appreciate the Cineteca di Bologna, a famous film archive and center for film restoration and research.

MAMbo: The Museum of Modern Art (MAMbo) in the University District is a must-visit for contemporary art lovers, showing a diverse range of modern artworks.

Bookstores and Cafés

Libreria Coop Ambasciatori: This historic bookstore is a treasure trove of books, including academic texts, classic literature, and current publications.

Café Culture: The University District is dotted with charming cafés, where you can enjoy a coffee or aperitivo while soaking yourself in the intellectual and artistic spirit of the neighborhood.

Preserving Academic Heritage

The University District serves as a living testament to the enduring heritage of education and scholarship in Bologna. The neighborhood's timeless draw lies in its ability to seamlessly blend tradition and innovation, nurturing the intellectual curiosity of students and tourists alike.

As you explore the University District of Bologna, you'll be captivated by the lively atmosphere, rich cultural offerings, and the profound impact of academic pursuits. The district's fusion of history, youthful exuberance, and foreign connections forms a unique tapestry that celebrates the essence of university life.

5.3 Santo Stefano

Welcome to the picturesque district of Santo Stefano, where ancient legends, spiritual heritage, and architectural wonders meet! This ancient neighborhood is home to the magnificent Basilica di Santo Stefano, a complex of seven churches and chapels, each with its unique charm and history. Let's discover the captivating details of Santo Stefano:

Basilica di Santo Stefano

The Seven Churches: The Basilica di Santo Stefano, also known as the Seven Churches, is a cluster of religious buildings that form one of Bologna's most important religious sites. The complex goes back to the 5th century and has been a place of pilgrimage for centuries.

The Church of the Crucifix: This is the first church you meet, and it features a beautiful crucifix, as well as stunning medieval frescoes and mosaics.

The Church of San Vitale and Agricola: Dedicated to two Christian martyrs, this church houses a rare collection of Byzantine-style mosaics.

The Courtyard: The tranquil courtyard between the churches is adorned with elegant porticoes and a central well, giving a serene space for reflection and contemplation.

Legends and Lore

The Well of the Pilate: According to local legends, the well in the courtyard is known as the Well of the Pilate, as it is thought to have been used to wash Pontius Pilate's hands.

The Whispering Columns: Inside the Church of San Vitale and Agricola, you'll find two marble columns with the ability to carry words across the church. Embrace the mystical air and try it out for yourself!

The Ancient Origins

Roman Foundations: The Basilica di Santo Stefano is built upon the remains of old Roman buildings, including a temple dedicated to the goddess Isis. As you explore the complex, you'll meet layers of history that span millennia.

Piazza Santo Stefano

Vibrant Gathering Place: Piazza Santo Stefano is a charming square close to the basilica, bustling with life. Cafés, shops, and neighborhood vendors add to the vibrant atmosphere.

Festive Celebrations: The square hosts different cultural events, markets, and festive gatherings throughout the year, creating a sense of community and joy.

Archaeological Discoveries

Museo Civico Archeologico: Just a short walk from Santo Stefano, you'll find the Museo Civico Archeologico, housing a rich collection of archaeological artifacts from past civilizations, including the Etruscans and Romans.

Preserving the Spiritual Heritage

Santo Stefano is a testament to Bologna's profound spiritual heritage and its historical significance as a spiritual pilgrimage place for visitors from across the world.

As you wander through Santo Stefano, you'll be transported back in time to an era of ancient tales and sacred wonders. The basilica's timeless beauty and spiritual aura create a sense of awe and respect, leaving you with an unforgettable experience of Bologna's rich historical and cultural tapestry.

5.4 Bolognina

Welcome to the lively and diverse neighborhood of Bolognina, a melting pot of cultures and a hub of creativity! Located just outside the historic city center, Bolognina offers a unique blend of tradition and modernity, making it a fascinating place to discover. Let's dig into the captivating details of Bolognina:

Multicultural Melting Pot

A Welcoming Community: Bolognina is known for its multicultural atmosphere, as it is home to a diverse population from different backgrounds and cultures. This vibrant mix of countries adds a unique flavor to the neighborhood.

Local Markets: Visit the lively open-air markets, such as Mercato della Piazzola and Mercato di Via Albani, where you'll find an array of fresh produce, local delicacies, and foreign spices and ingredients.

Street Art and Urban Creativity

Open-Air Gallery: Bolognina is a haven for street art and urban innovation. As you stroll through the streets, you'll meet colorful murals, graffiti, and art installations that reflect the neighborhood's dynamic spirit.

Exhibitions and Events: Keep an eye out for art exhibitions, performances, and cultural events held in the various galleries and alternative spaces in Bolognina. This area is a breeding ground for artistic expression.

Historical Landmarks

Porticoes and Architecture: Bolognina boasts elegant porticoed streets and historic buildings that mix with modern constructions. Take a leisurely walk along Via Matteotti and Via Mascarella to watch this architectural fusion.

Chiesa di San Rocco: This charming church in Bolognina features a striking neoclassical entrance and houses valuable religious artworks.

Local Flavors

Traditional Trattorias: Explore the trattorias and osterias in Bolognina, where you can indulge in traditional Bolognese dishes and local favorites. Don't miss out on trying tagliatelle al ragù or pasta in brodo.

Ethnic Cuisine: Bolognina also offers a wide range of international dining choices, including Middle Eastern, Asian, and African restaurants. It's a gastronomic adventure for those wanting diverse flavors.

Community Spaces

Parco del Cavaticcio: This pleasant park offers a green oasis for locals and visitors to relax and enjoy the outdoors. It's an ideal spot for picnics and relaxed strolls.

Centro Sociale XM24: This social center is a symbol of Bolognina's grassroots activism and community involvement. It offers cultural events, workshops, and discussions, offering a platform for social and political dialogue.

Urban Regeneration

Revitalization Efforts: Bolognina has undergone major urban regeneration in recent years, breathing new life into its public spaces, squares, and buildings.

Community Projects: Local residents are heavily involved in community projects that aim to improve the neighborhood's social fabric and enhance its livability.

Embracing Diversity

Bolognina welcomes its diversity and serves as a vibrant testament to the spirit of inclusion and openness that defines Bologna. This neighborhood's welcoming atmosphere and creative energy make it a must-visit destination for those wanting an authentic and dynamic experience.

As you explore Bolognina, you'll uncover the soul of a neighborhood that thrives on diversity, creativity, and community involvement. From its colorful street art to its rich culinary scene, Bolognina offers an immersive and enriching journey through the diverse facets of Bologna's modern urban setting.

5.5 San Donato

Welcome to San Donato, a charming neighborhood that mixes history, culture, and local charm! Located just outside the city's ancient walls, San Donato offers a delightful escape from the bustling city center while keeping its unique character. Let's discover the captivating details of San Donato:

Historical Roots

Medieval Origin: San Donato has medieval beginnings and was once an independent village before becoming part of Bologna. Its rich history is obvious in the architecture and layout of the neighborhood.

Porta San Donato: This iconic gate is one of Bologna's ancient city gates, going back to the 13th century. It served as one of the main entry places into the city and remains a historical landmark.

Santuario di San Luca

Breathtaking Panorama: San Donato is home to the famous Santuario di San Luca, an iconic basilica that sits atop a hill facing the city. Visitors can reach the sanctuary by walking along the famous Portico di San Luca, a covered arcade running over 3.5 kilometers (about 2.2 miles).

Pilgrimage Site: The Santuario di San Luca holds great religious significance and is a popular location for pilgrims and tourists alike. The breathtaking panoramic views from the hilltop make the trip even more rewarding.

Local Traditions

Fiera di San Donato: San Donato hosts the annual Fiera di San Donato, a lively street fair that takes place in October. During this event, the neighborhood comes alive with stalls, entertainment, and cultural celebrations.

Community Spirit: San Donato has a strong sense of community, and its people take pride in preserving local traditions and fostering a close-knit neighborhood atmosphere.

Hidden Gems

Via degli Orti: Explore Via degli Orti, a picturesque street lined with quaint houses, small gardens, and colorful paintings. It offers a glimpse into the local way of life and provides a serene break from the city's hustle and bustle.

House delle Rose: This historic house is surrounded by a beautiful park, providing a peaceful retreat where you can enjoy nature and perhaps have a relaxing picnic.

Authentic Flavors

Local Eateries: San Donato is home to a variety of cozy trattorias and pizzerias, where you can savor traditional Bolognese food in a relaxed and welcoming ambiance.

Genuine Hospitality: The neighborhood's friendly locals will make you feel right at home, and you'll likely experience the warm hospitality that defines the spirit of Bologna.

Preserving Local Identity

San Donato is a living testament to Bologna's deep-rooted past and its ability to embrace modernity while preserving its local character. This charming neighborhood welcomes you to step back in time and experience the authentic spirit of Bologna.

As you venture through San Donato, you'll be enchanted by its historical sites, scenic views, and genuine sense of community. The Santuario di San Luca and the neighborhood's warm hospitality make San Donato a memorable and enriching stop in Bologna.

5.6 Other Interesting Neighborhoods

Beyond the well-known districts, Bologna is dotted with a variety of fascinating neighborhoods, each with its own unique character and charm. These lesser-explored areas offer unique experiences that add depth to your trip through the city. Let's find some of Bologna's other interesting neighborhoods:

Navile

Modern and Multicultural: Navile is a dynamic neighborhood known for its modern architecture, multicultural vibe, and colorful street art. It is home to a diverse society and offers a glimpse into contemporary Bologna.

Saragozza

Historical Heritage: Saragozza is a historical neighborhood that swirls around the majestic Basilica di San Luca. Its cobbled streets, historic buildings, and charming atmosphere make it a delightful place to explore.

Portico di San Luca: Embark on the iconic Portico di San Luca, a covered arcade that runs for over 3.5 kilometers (about 2.2 miles) and leads up to the Santuario di San Luca atop Colle della Guardia. The panoramic views along the portico are a highlight of the trip.

Murri and Rizzoli

Art and Literature: These neighborhoods are linked with the intellectual heritage of Bologna. Explore the murals dedicated to famous author and screenwriter Pier Paolo Pasolini, who had strong ties to the city.

Libreria Nanni: Visit Libreria Nanni, a unique bookstore and cultural center, known for its focus on independent and alternative publishing.

Cirenaica

Industrial Charm: Cirenaica was originally an industrial area, and remnants of its industrial past can still be seen in its architecture. Today, the neighborhood is experiencing urban revitalization and transforming into a creative hub.

Mast Art District: Discover the Mast Art District, a cultural center that hosts art exhibitions, performances, and creative workshops, adding to the neighborhood's artistic rejuvenation.

Santo Stefano-Saragozza

Blending Heritage: This area is the intersection of the Santo Stefano and Saragozza neighborhoods, giving a captivating mix of historical landmarks and charming streets.

Palazzo Hercolani: Visit Palazzo Hercolani, a stunning building that houses the Museo della Musica, dedicated to the history of music in Bologna.

San Felice

Quaint Elegance: San Felice is a quaint and elegant neighborhood, exuding a relaxed environment. Its narrow streets, art galleries, and local shops create a picturesque ambiance.

Giardini di Scandellara: Stroll through the Giardini di Scandellara, a lovely garden that offers a tranquil area to unwind and enjoy nature.

Venturing into these lesser-known neighborhoods, you'll uncover hidden gems, experience contemporary culture, and meet unique aspects of Bologna's identity. Each area adds to the rich tapestry of the city, offering diverse and enriching experiences for travelers looking to delve deeper into Bologna's soul.

Hidden Gems and Off-the-Beaten-Path

6.1 Secret Courtyards and Gardens

Bologna is not only a city of grand landmarks and bustling squares but also a treasure trove of secret courtyards and tranquil gardens, tucked away behind ancient walls and unassuming entrances. These secret oases offer a respite from the city's vibrant streets and provide a chance to uncover hidden gems. Let's discover some of Bologna's enchanting secret courtyards and gardens:

Courtyard of Palazzo d'Accursio

A Historical Gem: Step into the Courtyard of Palazzo d'Accursio, a hidden gem nestled within the City Hall building. This enchanting courtyard boasts a harmonious blend of Renaissance and Gothic architecture, giving a glimpse into Bologna's rich history.

Ancient waterfall: Admire the central waterfall adorned with delicate sculptures and decorative elements, which has been a centerpiece of the area for centuries.

Courtyard of Palazzo Re Enzo

Medieval Splendor: Behind the imposing Palazzo Re Enzo, you'll find a delightful garden that reflects the grandeur of medieval Bologna. The courtyard's arches and colonnades create a captivating vibe.

Legends of Love: According to legend, the courtyard watched the passionate love story of Paolo and Francesca, immortalized by Dante in his Divine Comedy. Take a moment to immerse yourself in the romantic charm of this historic setting.

Orto Botanico di Bologna

Botanical Treasure: Escape to the Orto Botanico di Bologna, the city's botanical park, a serene haven hidden from the bustling streets. Founded in 1568, this lush park is an oasis of biodiversity and a living museum of plant life.

Plant Collections: Explore the varied collections of plants, including medicinal herbs, exotic species, and ancient trees. Don't miss the peaceful Japanese Garden, a sign of cultural exchange.

Courtyard of Santa Maria della Vita

Baroque Elegance: Enter the Courtyard of Santa Maria della Vita, an exquisite example of Baroque building nestled near the eponymous church. The courtyard's elegant porticoes and decorative elements evoke a feeling of timeless beauty.

Calm and Contemplation: The courtyard offers a peaceful respite where you can think on the intricate details and immerse yourself in the Baroque charm.

Corte Isolani

Medieval Oasis: Discover the secret courtyard of Corte Isolani, a medieval gem tucked away in the heart of the city. Surrounded by historic buildings, this quaint garden exudes an aura of antiquity.

Art and Culture: Corte Isolani is not only an architectural delight but also hosts art shows and cultural events, adding to the artistic ambiance.

Giardini Margherita

Urban Escape: While not entirely hidden, Giardini Margherita offers a vast expanse of greenery and is a favorite among locals wanting an urban escape. Its sheer size allows you to find peaceful corners away from the main roads.

Lake and Boat Rentals: Enjoy a leisurely stroll around the lake, take a boat, or simply sit by the water's edge and soak in the tranquil surroundings.

Uncovering Bologna's secret courtyards and gardens shows the city's intimate side, where history, art, and nature intertwine to create unique and magical experiences. These hidden gems invite you to slow down, explore at your own pace, and enjoy the hidden wonders of this captivating city.

6.2 Quirky Museums and Exhibits

Bologna is not only a city of classic art and history but also a haven for quirky and offbeat museums and exhibits, offering a delightful twist to your culture exploration. These unique attractions praise eccentricity, creativity, and unusual themes. Let's dive into some of Bologna's most interesting quirky museums and exhibits:

Museum of the History of Bologna (Museo della Storia di Bologna)

Underground Adventure: Descend into the depths of Bologna's history with a visit to the underground part of the Museum of the History of Bologna. This exhibit takes you on a captivating trip through the city's ancient archaeological remains and medieval foundations.

Piazza Maggiore: Then and Now: Explore the area dedicated to Piazza Maggiore's evolution over the centuries, where multimedia displays and interactive installations bring the square's rich history to life.

Museum of the History of Bologna - Medieval Kitchen (Museo della Storia di Bologna - Cucina Medievale)

Taste of the Past: Step into a medieval kitchen setting where you can immerse yourself in the culinary customs of Bologna's past. This unique exhibit showcases ancient cooking utensils, recipes, and food preparation techniques, giving a taste of history.

Interactive Experience: Engage your senses by participating in interactive tasks, such as grinding spices or kneading dough, as you uncover the culinary delights of the Middle Ages.

Gelato Museum Carpigiani

Sweet Adventure: Delve into the interesting world of gelato at the Gelato Museum Carpigiani. Learn about the past of this beloved frozen treat and discover the secrets behind gelato making.

Tasting Sessions: The museum offers gelato taste sessions where you can savor an array of delicious flavors, both classic and innovative.

Palazzo Pepoli - Museum of the History of Bologna (Palazzo Pepoli - Museo della Storia di Bologna)

Virtual Time Travel: Palazzo Pepoli takes you on a captivating journey through Bologna's past with its immersive and interactive exhibits. From ancient times to the present day, this museum gives a unique blend of tradition and modernity.

Urban Exploration: Wander through a life-sized reconstruction of medieval Bologna, filled with historic buildings and scenes that transport you back in time.

The Museum of Wax Anatomy (Museo di Anatomia Patologica dell'Università di Bologna)

Anatomical Curiosities: This fascinating yet peculiar museum houses a collection of wax models that show various pathological conditions. The museum played a major role in medical education during the 18th and 19th centuries.

Historic Medical Art: The intricately crafted wax models provide a glimpse into the medical practices and knowledge of earlier ages, making it a thought-provoking experience.

San Colombano - Collezione Tagliavini

Musical Marvels: This unique museum showcases a vast collection of musical instruments from different historical eras and cultures. From old lyres to Renaissance lutes and exotic instruments, it's a symphony of musical history.

Musical Demonstrations: The museum occasionally hosts live musical performances, allowing visitors to watch the instruments in action and experience the enchanting melodies they produce.

Exploring Bologna's quirky museums and exhibits is an adventure in itself, giving a delightful departure from traditional cultural experiences. These offbeat attractions are a testament to the city's creativity, curiosity, and passion for preserving unique aspects of its history.

6.3 Local Artisans and Shops

Bologna's lively artisan scene is a treasure trove of craftsmanship, creativity, and unique souvenirs. Exploring the city's local artisans and shops allows you to connect with the rich traditions and modern artistry that define Bologna. Here are some must-visit places to discover the works of skilled artisans:

Via dell'Indipendenza

Shopping Promenade: Start your journey along Via dell'Indipendenza, one of Bologna's main shopping streets. Here, you'll find a mix of well-known brands and charming boutiques selling clothing, accessories, and locally made goods.

Local Artisans' Showcase: Keep an eye out for shops that proudly show "Made in Bologna" products, as they often feature items crafted by local artisans.

Via Clavature and Via Pescherie Vecchie

Craftsmanship Galore: Stroll through the narrow streets of Via Clavature and Via Pescherie Vecchie, which are teeming with craft workshops and boutique stores.

Leather Goods: Bologna is famous for its leather craftsmanship. Visit specialized shops that offer exquisite leather goods, from handbags and wallets to belts and accessories.

Ceramics and Pottery

Via Cartoleria: This charming street is famous for its handmade ceramics and pottery shops. Discover beautifully handmade tableware, decorative items, and unique souvenirs.

Bottega Artigiana del Libro: If you enjoy the art of bookbinding, visit this workshop to watch skilled artisans creating intricate leather-bound books and journals.

Traditional Food Delights

Mercato di Mezzo: This busy market in the heart of Bologna is a paradise for foodies. Explore the stalls and taste local treats like Parmigiano-Reggiano cheese, traditional cured meats, and regional wines.

Salumeria Simoni: Step into this renowned salumeria (delicatessen) to taste some of the finest local cured meats and gourmet products. The shopkeepers are often happy to share stories and tips.

Jewelry and Artisanal Accessories

Via Augusto Righi: This street is home to various jewelry shops and artisanal boutiques, offering a diverse selection of handcrafted pieces, from modern designs to antique-inspired treasures.

Boutiques and Concept Stores: Explore the concept stores that feature a curated selection of unique accessories and lifestyle products, great for finding one-of-a-kind souvenirs.

La Piazzola Market

Flea Market Finds: Visit La Piazzola, a lively flea market held on weekends near Piazza VIII Agosto. Here, you'll discover vintage gems, antiques, and quirky collectibles.

Bargain Hunting: Don't be afraid to haggle with the friendly sellers for the best deals on your favorite finds.

Immerse yourself in Bologna's artisanal charm and take home memories in the form of unique, handcrafted gifts that reflect the city's creativity and artistry. Supporting local artisans also helps to preserve Bologna's cultural history and vibrant community of craftsmen.

6.4 Unexplored Neighborhoods

Beyond the well-trodden tourist paths, Bologna hides a world of unexplored areas, where the true essence of the city's daily life and local culture can be experienced. These lesser-known areas offer a chance to delve deeper into Bologna's soul and find hidden treasures. Let's journey into some of Bologna's unexplored neighborhoods:

San Donato-San Vitale

Historical Gems: This area, located to the east of the city center, is brimming with historical landmarks and lesser-known sights.

Portico di San Luca (Partial): While the beginning of the iconic Portico di San Luca is well-known, going further along the portico offers a less crowded and equally stunning experience.

Parco della Chiusa: This lovely park offers a quiet escape and a chance to relax amidst lush greenery and historic ruins.

Bolognina-San Donato

Creative Vibe: Bolognina is an up-and-coming area known for its artistic flair and diverse community.

Mast Art District: This cultural center hosts art exhibitions, performances, and creative events that highlight the neighborhood's contemporary and artistic energy.

Museum of Industrial Heritage (Museo del Patrimonio Industriale): Uncover the industrial past of Bologna in this fascinating museum, housed in a former factory.

Murri-Reno

Local Charm: Murri-Reno, located in the eastern part of Bologna, offers a glimpse into the authentic daily life of the locals.

Borgo della Salute: Stroll through this historic area, known for its lively markets, traditional shops, and bright atmosphere.

Parco Cavaioni: Embrace nature in Parco Cavaioni, a peaceful park with walking trails and green areas perfect for a leisurely afternoon.

San Ruffillo-San Donnino

Offbeat and Serene: This quiet area to the west of the city center offers a tranquil break from the urban hustle.

Villa Angeletti: Discover the historic Villa Angeletti, a beautiful house surrounded by a lovely park, providing a serene setting for a leisurely walk.

Botanical Garden (Partial): While the main Orto Botanico is popular, exploring the lesser-known sections offers a quieter experience among rare and exotic plants.

Colli-Belvedere

Panoramic Views: The Colli-Belvedere area is known for its wide views of Bologna's skyline.

San Michele in Bosco: Visit the beautiful Basilica of San Michele in Bosco, perched on a hill, offering stunning views of the city.

Villa Ghigi: This expansive park is great for nature lovers, hikers, and those wanting breathtaking vistas.

Unexplored neighborhoods grant you the opportunity to witness Bologna's authentic essence and find lesser-known wonders that enrich your travel experience. Immerse yourself in the local rhythms, and embrace the city's hidden corners to create lasting memories of your trip through Bologna.

Food and Dining

7.1. Introduction to Bolognese Cuisine

Prepare your taste buds for an unforgettable culinary trip as you delve into the heart of Bolognese cuisine, a gastronomic tradition deeply rooted in history and passion. Bologna, often referred to as "La Grassa" (The Fat One), takes immense pride in its rich food heritage, which has shaped the way Italians and food enthusiasts worldwide view the art of cooking. Let's experience the delightful world of Bolognese cuisine:

The Art of Simplicity

Quality Ingredients: Bolognese food revolves around the use of fresh and high-quality ingredients. From locally sourced vegetables to the finest meats, each dish welcomes simplicity and authenticity.

Emphasis on Flavor: The attention is on enhancing the natural flavors of the ingredients, allowing each element to shine through without excessive embellishment.

Iconic Dishes

Tagliatelle al Ragù: Perhaps the most popular dish from Bologna, this is not your ordinary spaghetti with meat sauce. Tagliatelle, a ribbon-like pasta, is lovingly dressed with a slow-cooked ragù sauce made from soft meat, tomatoes, and aromatic herbs.

Tortellini in Brodo: These delectable, handmade pasta parcels are filled with a mixture of meats, cheese, and spices. Served in a thick and savory broth, they provide comfort and warmth on chilly days.

Lasagna Bolognese: Layers of fresh pasta sheets, creamy béchamel sauce, and rich meat ragù combine to make this heavenly comfort food that leaves a lasting impression.

Meat Heaven

Bolognese Meats: The city's meat-based meals are a testament to the exceptional quality of the region's meats, which include pork, beef, and veal. Whether it's in a sumptuous pasta sauce or a succulent grilled dish, Bologna shows its prowess in meat preparation.

Salumi: Bologna is a salumi lover's dream. Try Mortadella, the ancestor of modern-day bologna, or try the savory delights of Prosciutto di Parma and Culatello.

Cheese Delights

Parmigiano-Reggiano: The "King of Cheeses" hails from the area surrounding Bologna. Savoring aged Parmigiano-Reggiano is a must, and you can find it grated over pasta or placed on a platter with traditional balsamic vinegar.

Mozzarella di Bufala: Although not local to Bologna, this luscious buffalo milk cheese is widely enjoyed throughout Italy, and you can find it featured in many recipes.

Traditional Flavors

Balsamic Vinegar: From nearby Modena, traditional balsamic vinegar elevates many meals with its deep, complex flavors. Drizzle it over Parmigiano-Reggiano or strawberries for a unique taste.

Tigelle and Crescentine: These round, soft bread discs are great for savoring with cured meats, cheeses, and spreads.

Aperitivo Culture

Evening Ritual: Experience the Bolognese aperitivo culture, where locals meet at bars for pre-dinner drinks and indulge in a spread of appetizers, ranging from olives and cheeses to various finger foods.

Sweets and Desserts

Torta di Riso: A unique rice cake flavored with citrus and cinnamon, making it a delightful treat with a history going back to the Middle Ages.

Zuppa Inglese: This Italian dessert is similar to English trifle, having layers of sponge cake, custard, and a hint of Alchermes liqueur.

Bolognese food celebrates the harmony of simplicity and quality, captivating your senses with unforgettable flavors and culinary artistry. As you visit the city's restaurants, trattorias, and osterias, you'll savor the love and passion that goes into each dish, leaving you with an enduring appreciation for the magic of Bolognese cooking.

7.2. Must-Try Dishes and Local Specialties

Bologna's culinary repertoire is a delightful tapestry of flavors, offering a myriad of must-try dishes and local favorites that will tantalize your taste buds and leave you craving for more. From the iconic classics to lesser-known gems, each dish represents a unique facet of Bolognese food. Get ready to start on a gastronomic adventure as you savor these delectable offerings:

1. Tagliatelle al Ragù

A Timeless Classic: The uncontested star of Bolognese cooking, Tagliatelle al Ragù is a meal you just cannot miss. Long, flat ribbons of egg pasta are skillfully coated in a sumptuous ragù sauce, slow-cooked with tender meat, aromatic veggies, and a touch of tomato.

Authentic Presentation: To experience the full spirit of this meal, enjoy it in a classic trattoria where the pasta is freshly prepared and the ragù has simmered for hours, getting the ideal harmony of flavors.

2. Tortellini en Brodo

Comfort in a Bowl: This cozy meal combines delicate tortellini stuffed with a delectable blend of meats and cheese, served in a clear, savory broth. The easiness and heartiness of Tortellini en Brodo make it a great choice throughout the colder months.

Handmade Craftsmanship: Witness the talent of artists as they mold each tiny tortellini by hand, a procedure that has been passed down through generations.

3. Lasagna Bolognese

Layers of Love: Lasagna Bolognese is a labor of love, with thin pasta sheets sandwiched between silky béchamel sauce and a thick, savory meat ragù. This dish is a symphony of flavors and textures, providing a harmonious treat.

Homestyle Indulgence: Many family-run trattorias serve their own cherished version of lasagna, expressing the love and tradition of home-cooked meals.

4. Bollito Misto

Boiled Beauty: Bollito Misto is a potpourri of boiled meats, including beef, veal, and chicken, served with a range of sauces such as salsa verde and mostarda. This dish displays the beauty of simplicity, where the quality of the meats takes center stage.

Elegant Accompaniments: It's normal to find a dish of Bollito Misto accompanied by a variety of veggies, such as potatoes, carrots, and cabbage, offering a balanced and fulfilling meal.

5. Crescentine

Hearty Fare: Crescentine, also known as tigelle, are small, round, and somewhat puffy bread discs, perfect for filling with cured meats, cheeses, and spreads. This rustic treat is a popular among locals for its simplicity and adaptability.

Traditionally Local: Crescentine are strongly anchored in the culinary legacy of the Emilia-Romagna area, and tasting them is a lovely way to experience an important component of Bolognese culture.

6. Mortadella

The Original Bologna: Mortadella is the forefather of the well-known bologna sausage and a municipal specialty. This big, delicate, and lightly seasoned sausage has a distinct flavor that demonstrates the expertise of local producers.

Look for artisanal butchers who take delight in preparing their own mortadella using traditional processes and excellent ingredients.

7. English Spaghetti

Sweet Finish: Zuppa Inglese is a decadent Italian dessert reminiscent of English trifles. Layers of sponge cake, creamy custard, and a hint of Alchermes liqueur combine to create a symphony of flavors and textures.

A Long History: Zuppa Inglese has a long history in Bologna, and a slice is a delectable way to end a wonderful meal.

Bologna's must-try meals and regional delicacies are an invitation to taste the city's culinary craftsmanship and cultural legacy, with each bite telling a narrative of tradition and passion. You'll discover the heart and soul of Bolognese cuisine as you indulge in these culinary delicacies, leaving you with a great respect for the gastronomic treasures that await in this food lover's paradise.

7.3. Restaurants, Osterias, and Trattorias at Their Finest

The culinary scene in Bologna is a feast for the senses, with a variety of restaurants, osterias, and trattorias, each with its own distinct character and wonderful meals. Whether you're looking for Michelin-starred sophistication, traditional osteria atmosphere, or homey trattoria comfort, the city provides something for everyone. Here are some of the top places to eat Bolognese food:

1. Restaurant Osteria dell'Orsa

Osteria dell'Orsa is a renowned institution known for its warm and inviting ambiance. With its home-cooked Bolognese staples and ample quantities, this lively osteria attracts both residents and tourists.

Must-Try Dish: Tagliatelle al Ragù, a delectable interpretation of the famed Bolognese pasta.

2. Anna Maria Trattoria

Trattoria Anna Maria has been family-owned and operated since 1985. It takes pride in serving traditional Bolognese dishes handed down through generations.

Don't miss their Tortellini en Brodo, a soul-satisfying dish that embodies the spirit of Bolognese comfort food.

3. The Serghei Trattoria

Trattoria Serghei, located near the University, has a rich history and a beautiful setting. Its rustic design and helpful employees make a welcoming environment.

House Specialty: The Bollito Misto, a variety of boiled meats paired with delectable sauces, is a house specialty.

4. Da Cesari's

Da Cesari is well-known for its excellent dining experience and culinary quality. Since 1955, the restaurant has served delectable Bolognese cuisine.

Signature Dish: Try their Cotoletta alla Bolognese, which is a breaded and fried veal cutlet that will leave you wanting more.

5. The Pappagallo Restaurant

Ristorante Pappagallo is located in a historic edifice that emanates luxury and sophistication. Its exquisite menu showcases the best of Bolognese and Italian cuisine.

Gastronomic trip: Choose their tasting menu to go on a culinary trip through the flavors of Bologna.

6. Gianni Trattoria

Trattoria da Gianni is a family-run trattoria known for delivering delectable dishes created from locally sourced products.

Seasonal Offerings: The menu changes with the seasons to ensure that you get the freshest ingredients all year.

7. Gold Caminetto

Caminetto d'Oro is a Michelin-starred restaurant that takes Bolognese cuisine to new heights with inventive and elegantly presented meals.

Innovative Flavors: Let the talented chef surprise you with a tasting menu of innovative variations on traditional Bolognese specialities.

The top restaurants, osterias, and trattorias in Bologna highlight the city's culinary tradition and enthusiasm for fine food, providing a unique dining experience that you will remember long after your visit. You'll understand why Bologna is a destination that captivates food fans from all over the world as you taste the rich flavors and warm warmth of these places.

7.4. Options for Vegans and Vegetarians

Bologna is famous for its meat-centric cuisine, but the city has also embraced the growing demand for vegan and vegetarian food, providing a delectable array of plant-based options to suit a wide range of tastes. Bologna has something for everyone, whether you're a dedicated vegan or simply looking to eat lighter and healthier meals. Here are some excellent vegan and vegetarian places to try:

1. Vegano Universo

Vegan Fast Food: Universo Vegano is a well-known network of vegan fast-food restaurants. Vegetarian burgers, sandwiches, wraps, and salads are available, all created using plant-based components.

Must-Try Dish: Their vegan lasagna, cooked with rich tomato sauce and creamy plant-based béchamel, is a must-try.

2. Cucina Vegana Botanica Lab

Botanica Lab Cucina Vegana delivers unique and attractively presented vegan recipes that highlight the diversity of plant-based ingredients.

Recommendation: For a unique culinary experience, try their vegan sushi rolls and inventive vegetable-based entrees.

3. Restaurant Il Sole

Ristorante Il Sole is a fine vegan restaurant that caters to the most discriminating palates. The menu features exquisite vegan cuisine produced with the finest and freshest ingredients.

Signature Dish: Try their vegan Tagliatelle al Ragù, a culinary masterpiece that embodies the spirit of Bolognese cuisine.

4. Madame Sorelle

Le Sorelle is a quaint vegan pizzeria that serves a variety of tasty plant-based pizzas, including classics and inventive combos.

Must-Try Pizza: Try their "La Vegana" pizza, which comes topped with vegan cheese, seasonal vegetables, and delectable vegan sausage.

5. Orto

Orto is a farm-to-table vegan restaurant that emphasizes local and organic vegetables in its cuisine.

Seasonal Delights: The menu changes with the seasons, guaranteeing that you always get the freshest and most flavorful items.

6. VURS

Vegan Gelato: For a sweet treat, visit VURS, a vegan gelateria that serves a variety of plant-based gelato flavors produced with natural ingredients.

Gelato Indulgence: Enjoy classic flavors like chocolate and pistachio, or experiment with innovative vegan creations like lavender and raspberry sorbetto.

7. Terra and Luna

Vegan-Friendly Osteria: While not totally vegan, Terra e Luna is an osteria that serves vegan-friendly meals and accommodates dietary restrictions.

Warm Ambience: Enjoy a pleasant and friendly environment while eating their delectable vegan options.

Bologna's vegan and vegetarian scene is flourishing, demonstrating the city's commitment to embracing varied culinary options. Bologna caters to every taste and culinary philosophy, from delectable vegan gelato to gourmet plant-based delicacies.

7.5. Traditional Food Stores

Bologna's traditional food markets are a sensory feast, displaying the city's rich culinary culture as well as the finest produce from the surrounding Emilia-Romagna area. Exploring these markets provides an authentic and immersive experience, allowing you to connect with local vendors and discover the freshest ingredients that form the foundation of Bolognese cuisine. Here are some of Bologna's must-see historic food markets:

1. Mezzanine Market

Mercato di Mezzo, located in the heart of the city, is one of Bologna's oldest markets, dating back to medieval times. The market is a hive of activity, with stalls selling a delectable array of local goods.

Food Delights: As you meander through this historic marketplace, sample traditional cheeses, fresh fruits, cured meats, olives, and other regional specialties.

2. The Erbe Market

Local Treasure: Mercato delle Erbe is a bustling indoor market where locals and tourists alike come to buy fresh produce, meats, and artisanal goods.

Street Food Heaven: The market also has a number of food stalls and cafés, making it a great place to sample street food favorites like piadina, panini, and fresh pasta dishes.

3. Market Quadrilatero

Historical Charm: Quadrilatero is a lovely neighborhood with a bustling street market. It's a maze of little lanes packed with traditional shops and vendors.

Bolognese Delights: Sample a variety of regional delicacies such as tortellini, Parmigiano-Reggiano, and balsamic vinegar.

4. Ritrovato Mercato

Farmers' Market: Every Friday afternoon in the scenic Piazza San Francesco, the Mercato Ritrovato hosts a vibrant farmers' market.

Taste the freshness of locally grown fruits and vegetables, artisan cheeses, organic meats, and freshly baked goodies.

5. Nettuno's Market

Mercato del Nettuno is a renowned marketplace located near to the great Fountain of Neptune.

While it is well known for its fish market, it also has stalls offering regional items such as prosciutto, salami, and freshly baked bread.

6. Eataly World FICO

FICO Eataly World is an outstanding food-themed park dedicated to Italian cooking. It's an immersive experience in which you may explore numerous culinary pavilions and learn about traditional Italian food manufacturing.

Taste of Italy: In this gastronomic wonderland, sample regional specialties from all over Italy, including Bologna's famous cuisine.

Bologna's ancient food markets are a culinary treasure trove, providing a window into the city's gastronomic spirit. These markets promise a memorable and savory experience, whether you're looking for fresh supplies to prepare your own meals or anxious to enjoy real local specialties.

7.6. Bologna's Wine and Aperitivo Culture

The wine and aperitivo culture of Bologna adds a pleasurable and social layer to the city's culinary scene, allowing visitors to appreciate both the rich flavors of regional wines and a broad assortment of appetizers. As the sun sets over Bologna, the city comes alive with inhabitants and tourists congregating at pubs and restaurants to engage in the cherished Italian tradition of aperitivo. Everything you need to know about Bologna's wine culture and the art of aperitivo is right here:

1. The Wine Tradition of Bolognese

Pignoletto: Bologna's most famous wine, Pignoletto is a crisp and delightful sparkling white wine. It's ideal for aperitivo snacks and light dinners.

Sangiovese: This red wine variety is well-known throughout Emilia-Romagna. Its rich, fruity flavor complements substantial Bolognese recipes.

2. Wine Bars and Enotecas

Enoteca Italiana: Enoteca Italiana, located in the centre of Bologna, provides a broad selection of Italian wines. It's a great place to sample a variety of regional and local wines.

Wine Bars: Strolling through the city's lovely streets will lead you to various wine bars (enoteche) where you may have a glass of wine and light nibbles.

3. Ritual of Aperitivo

Evening ritual: Aperitivo is a beloved Italian ritual served before dinner, where friends and coworkers congregate for drinks and nibbles.

Aperitivo Hotspots: Piazza Santo Stefano, Via del Pratello, and Via Zamboni are renowned aperitivo hotspots.

4. Aperitivo Selections

Buffet Style: In Bologna, aperitivo is frequently served as a buffet, with bars and restaurants laying out a selection of finger appetizers and starters.

Apericena: Aperitivo can be so bountiful that it becomes a light dinner, hence the name "apericena."

5. Snacks for an Aperitivo

Bruschetta: A popular Italian snack made of toasted bread topped with fresh tomatoes, garlic, and olive oil.

Crostini are small, toasted bread pieces with savory toppings such as pâté, cheese, and vegetables.

Olives and nuts are frequently served as a simple and pleasant addition to drinks.

6. Liqueurs with a Bitter Aftertaste

Amaro: This herbal liquor is a staple of aperitivo culture. Enjoy it neat or in cocktails like the Negroni and Spritz.

Aperol Spritz: This famous and pleasant drink is made with Aperol, prosecco, and soda.

7. Terzi's Coffee Shop

Caffè Terzi is well-known for its excellent coffee throughout the day and modern aperitivo offers in the evening.

Coffee Culture: Bologna is fanatical about coffee, and you may sample a range of espresso-based drinks across the city.

Bologna's wine and aperitivo culture is an integral element of the city's social fabric, inviting you to feel the warmth of Italian hospitality and delight in the region's delicacies. Whether you enjoy sipping local wines or socializing over aperitivo appetizers, these activities provide a fascinating and immersive way to experience the soul of Bologna.

Bologna shopping

8.1. Popular Shopping Districts and Streets

Shopping in Bologna is a treat, with a mix of modern businesses, artisanal shops, and historic markets catering to a wide range of tastes and interests. As you stroll around the city's lovely streets, you'll come across one-of-a-kind treasures ranging from high-end couture to local handicrafts. Here are some of the most prominent retail streets and districts in Bologna that you should not miss:

1. The Independence Way

Via dell'Indipendenza is Bologna's main retail street, buzzing with a mix of well-known names and small boutiques.

Fashion & More: As you go along this lively street, you'll come across a variety of fashion businesses, booksellers, and cafes.

2. Cavour Galleria

Galleria Cavour is Bologna's premium shopping area, including luxury brands and high-end stores.

Italian Elegance: If you're looking for designer clothing, jewelry, or high-end cosmetics, here is the place to go for a sumptuous shopping experience.

3. Rizzoli Street

Via Rizzoli is another prominent street in Bologna, with historical buildings and a variety of shopping alternatives.

Books & More: There are various bookstores on this street, plus apparel stores and gift shops cater to a wide range of customers.

4. Using Clavature

Via Clavature is a lovely street lined with artisanal stores providing handcrafted crafts, jewelry, and one-of-a-kind gifts.

Discover one-of-a-kind pieces that highlight the skill and creativity of local artists.

5. Mezzanine Market

Market Shopping: Mercato di Mezzo is a historical marketplace that also has contemporary shops and speciality food businesses.

Foodie Heaven: Bring home gourmet foods such as cheeses, cured meats, and balsamic vinegar to savour the flavors of Bologna.

6. The Erbe Market

Mercato delle Erbe has modest businesses providing clothing, accessories, and household items in addition to fresh fruit.

Aperitivo Stop: This is an excellent spot to enjoy an aperitivo while learning about the local culture.

7. Quadrilatero

The Quadrilatero is a medieval area consisting with narrow streets and alleyways filled with modest shops and stores.

Hidden jewels: Explore the nooks for hidden jewels such as artisanal goods and antiques.

The shopping streets and neighborhoods of Bologna provide a broad and captivating retail experience, with everything from high-fashion luxury items to one-of-a-kind handmade crafts. You'll find a treasure mine of shopping choices as you travel through the city's lovely neighborhoods, leaving you with lasting recollections of your time in Bologna.

8.2. Souvenirs and local products

Bringing original local goods and souvenirs from Bologna is a wonderful way to preserve your memories of the city and give a taste of its culture with loved ones. Bologna is known for its rich culinary history and artisanal skills, and it offers a wide range of one-of-a-kind and high-quality things. Here are a few must-have local items and souvenirs that encapsulate the soul of Bologna:

1. Cheese Parmigiano-Reggiano

King of Cheeses: Parmigiano-Reggiano, one of Italy's most recognized cheeses, is a must-have. Look for aged ones with nuanced flavors that are perfect for grating over pasta.

Local Delicacy: For the most authentic taste, use Parmigiano-Reggiano made in the surrounding area of Emilia-Romagna.

2. Balsamic Vinegar (Traditional)

Traditional balsamic vinegar from Modena, near Bologna, is a culinary treasure. Look for matured varieties with the designation Aceto Balsamico Tradizionale di Modena DOP.

Sweet and tangy: Add this delectable sauce on cheeses, salads, and even strawberries.

3. Mortadella

Bologna's Icon: Mortadella, the city's famed sausage, makes a tasty and one-of-a-kind souvenir.

Freshly Sliced: For the best flavor, buy it from a local deli or butcher shop, and serve it as part of a classic Italian antipasto.

4. Pasta cooked from scratch

Tagliatelle & Tortellini: Take home boxes of handmade tagliatelle and tortellini, Bolognese pasta's pride and joy.

Cooking Treasures: When prepared with the city's typical ragù sauce, these delicate pasta kinds provide a true taste of Bologna.

5. Pottery made by hand

Look for wonderfully produced ceramic objects that showcase Bologna's creative past.

Decorative and functional: Add a touch of Italian flair to your house with hand-painted plates, bowls, and tiles.

6. Souvenirs with an Opera Theme

Musical Connection: Bologna has a strong musical heritage as the cradle of opera.

Souvenirs from the Teatro Comunale di Bologna: Visit the Teatro Comunale di Bologna to find opera-themed souvenirs and products commemorating the city's musical past.

7. Instruments from the past

Accordion and mandolin: Buy traditional musical instruments to immerse yourself in Bologna's musical culture.

Music Shops: Look around the city for unique instruments that demonstrate Italy's love of music.

8. Scarves made of silk

Bologna is famous for its silk manufacture, and silk scarves make exquisite and sophisticated gifts.

Fashion Boutiques: Visit boutique boutiques to find a wide range of styles and colors, perfect for adding an Italian flair to your outfit.

Local items and souvenirs in Bologna are a lovely way to remember your stay and share the city's cultural assets with others. These treasured products, from the exquisite taste of Parmigiano-Reggiano to the beauty of artisanal pottery, bring a bit of Bologna's rich past into your life.

8.3. Antique and vintage item markets

Bologna is a treasure mine of antique and vintage markets and stores where you may look for one-of-a-kind and nostalgic items. These markets will enchant you with their broad assortment of timeless objects, whether you're looking for vintage apparel, souvenirs, or unique antiques. Here are some of the top spots in Bologna to look for antiques and vintage items:

1. Città Antiquario Mercato

Historic Antiques Market: Mercato Antiquario di Città, located in the center of the city, is Bologna's principal antique market.

Timeless Treasures: Peruse a unique collection of antique furniture, vintage jewelry, ancient books, and oddities from many eras.

Market Schedule: The market is normally held on the second Sunday of each month, although it's wise to double-check the times ahead of time.

2. The Quadrilatero Antiquariato Market

Quadrilatero's Hidden Gems: This little and quaint antique market is tucked away in the Quadrilatero region.

Discoveries: Browse the stalls for vintage postcards, retro items, and other delightful trinkets.

Market Dates: The market is typically held on the third Sunday of the month.

3. Ciambellano Market Place

Mercatino del Ciambellano is well-known for its eclectic mix of antiques and art.

Discover paintings, sculptures, prints, and other works of art that will add a touch of refinement to your collection.

Market Dates: The market is normally held on the fourth Sunday of each month.

4. The Pratello Street

Via del Pratello, a lively street in Bologna, is home to a variety of vintage and second-hand shops.

Vintage Fashion: Explore the world of retro fashion at these stores, which sell a variety of vintage apparel and accessories.

Keep an eye out for little shops that may have surprising treasures.

5. Market of the Pulci

Mercatino delle Pulci is a flea market where you may look for pre-loved items and antiques.

This market provides an unusual mix of vintage goodies, ranging from old vinyl records to retro home furnishings.

Market Schedule: The market is often held on Saturdays, although it is best to confirm the dates ahead of time.

Bologna's antique and vintage markets offer an insight into the city's rich history as well as an exciting opportunity to acquire unique and cherished objects from the past. These markets promise an amazing shopping experience, whether you're a seasoned collector or simply enjoy discovering nostalgic treasures.

8.4. Boutiques of Fashion and Design

Bologna is a fashion and design city with a vibrant mix of boutique boutiques and design shops catering to a wide range of preferences and trends. These shops and stores offer an outstanding assortment of Italian and international brands, whether you're a fashion enthusiast, a design aficionado, or simply looking for unusual and attractive products. Here are some of the best fashion and design stores in Bologna:

1. Cavour Galleria

Galleria Cavour is a prominent shopping gallery that houses luxury fashion names as well as high-end retailers.

Fashion Houses: For a taste of Italian luxury, visit world-renowned names such as Gucci, Prada, and Louis Vuitton.

2. Farini Street

Via Farini is a popular street in Bologna that has a mix of high-fashion boutiques and boutique shops.

Discover one-of-a-kind designs by Italian fashion designers and rising stars.

3. Ceccarelli Manufacturing Company

Manifattura Ceccarelli is a well-known store that specializes in high-quality outerwear.

Their clothing showcase Italian craftsmanship, from classic trench coats to trendy parkas.

4. Gioielli Lebole

Elegant Jewelry: Lebole Gioielli is a boutique that specializes in magnificent jewelry that combines classic and modern styles.

Handcrafted Pieces: Take a look at their handcrafted necklaces, bracelets, and earrings, which are ideal for a special present or personal pleasure.

5. Monrif Boutique Hotels

Monrif Hotels, such as Grand Hotel Majestic "già Baglioni," frequently have beautiful boutiques on their grounds.

Fashion and Luxury: Browse these stores for carefully chosen collections of clothing, accessories, and home decor.

6. The Pelle Drogheria

Drogheria della Pelle specializes on high-quality leather items such as bags, wallets, and belts.

Italian Leather: Spoil yourself with a gorgeous Italian leather item that will last a lifetime.

7. Bologna Blanc

White Bologna is a trendy concept boutique that features avant-garde apparel and design.

Emerging Designers: Look here for cutting-edge fashion pieces by emerging designers.

8. Area Design Mercato delle Erbe

Design Showroom: The Mercato delle Erbe has a section reserved for design showrooms and ateliers.

Discover trendy furniture, home furnishings, and one-of-a-kind design pieces in this creative space.

Bologna's fashion boutiques and design stores provide an enthralling voyage into the world of Italian style and design, displaying a diverse range of options that represent the city's creative vitality and fashion-forward character. Whether you're seeking high-fashion elegance, artisanal workmanship, or modern design, the retail scene in Bologna will satisfy and inspire you.

Nightlife and entertainment

9.1 Theatres and Concert Halls

Bologna's dynamic entertainment and nightlife scene includes theatres and music venues where you can immerse yourself in the city's artistic past as well as present cultural offers. If you enjoy theatre, opera, concerts, or live music, Bologna boasts a range of venues to suit your artistic inclinations. Here are some of the city's best theaters and music venues:

1. Bologna Municipal Theatre

The Teatro Comunale di Bologna, usually known as the Teatro Comunale, is a prominent opera house famed for its opera and ballet performances.

Rich History: The theatre has a long and illustrious history that dates back to the 18th century, making it a recognizable cultural institution in Bologna.

2. Duse Theatre

Teatro Duse is a prominent location for theatrical performances such as dramas, comedies, and contemporary shows.

With a seating capacity of roughly 700, the theatre provides an intimate and immersive experience.

3. The Estragon Club

Estragon Club is a well-known venue for live music events, offering concerts ranging from rock and indie to electronic music.

Famous Acts: Many well-known national and international artists have performed at Estragon Club.

4. Manzoni Auditorium.

Auditorium Manzoni is a well-known venue for classical music performances such as chamber music concerts and recitals.

Acoustic Excellence: The auditorium's superb acoustics enhance both performers' and audiences' listening experiences.

5. Bentivoglio Cantina

Cantina Bentivoglio is a one-of-a-kind place where you can enjoy live jazz and blues artists.

Wine and Music: Enjoy the ambiance with a glass of wine while listening to soulful tunes.

6. Link

Link is a multifunctional venue that organizes a wide range of events, from live music concerts to DJ nights and cultural gatherings.

The venue's creative atmosphere attracts artists, musicians, and performers from a variety of fields.

7. Café Zanarini

Live Piano Music: Zanarini Café is a charming venue where you can drink your coffee or aperitivo while listening to live piano music.

The exquisite atmosphere of the café provides a classy backdrop for an evening of leisure and music.

Bologna's theatres and music venues provide an enthralling choice of artistic experiences, allowing you to witness great performances and immerse yourself in the city's cultural tapestry. Bologna's entertainment sector offers to enrich your stay with unique moments, from the grandeur of opera halls to the intimate appeal of live music venues.

9.2 Bars and Nightclubs

Bologna's nightlife is vibrant and diversified, with numerous nightclubs and pubs where you can dance, chat, and enjoy a wide range of drinks and music. Whether you like a relaxed pub setting or a busy dance floor, there is something for everyone in the city. Here are some of the best places to party and drink in Bologna:

1. Cassero LGBT+ Community Center

Cassero, a well-known LGBT+ center in Bologna, hosts themed parties, drag shows, and events that celebrate diversity and inclusivity.

Welcoming Environment: It's an excellent place to meet new people and immerse yourself in a welcoming atmosphere.

2. Sound Club Sottotetto

Sottotetto Sound Club is a well-known nightclub noted for its electronic and techno music events.

Underground Vibes: The club attracts local and international DJs, resulting in an underground music culture.

3. The Link Club

Eclectic Nights: Link Club is a multipurpose facility that transforms from a cultural place to a nightclub at night.

Live Music and DJs: In this innovative and energetic setting, enjoy live music acts, DJ sets, and themed parties.

4. Beer & Food Barazzo

Barazzo Beer & Food is a fashionable pub that serves a wide variety of craft beers and gourmet drinks.

Hip Hangout: It's a popular hangout for both residents and tourists due to its welcoming atmosphere and cool decor.

5. Bologna Baladin

Craft Beer Pioneers: Baladin is a well-known Italian craft beer brewery with a pub and cafe in Bologna.

Beer Varieties: For beer fans, explore a variety of artisan brews with distinct flavors.

6. Lab 16

Gin and Cocktails: Lab 16 is a chic gin bar specializing in one-of-a-kind cocktails and premium gins.

Mixology Delights: Enjoy the wonderful concoctions while watching experienced mixologists produce them.

7. Restaurant del Sole

Osteria del Sole, one of Bologna's oldest taverns, dates back to the 15th century.

Bring Your Own Food: It's a novel concept in which you can bring your own food and drink with friends in a convivial setting.

8. Pubs in Ireland and the United Kingdom

Pub Culture: There are various Irish and British pubs in Bologna that provide a flavor of home away from home.

Enjoy live sports broadcasts, live music sessions, and a variety of exotic beers.

The nightclubs and bars in Bologna cater to a broad population, making it simple to locate a location that suits your tastes. The city's nightlife has you covered whether you desire a night of dancing, a pleasant bar setting, or a place to connect with locals and fellow travelers.

9.3 Concerts and Live Music

Bologna's thriving music scene provides a diversified choice of live performances and concerts including a wide spectrum of musical styles and artists. You'll find places and events that appeal to your musical tastes, whether you like classical music, jazz, rock, or independent bands. Here are some of the best places in Bologna to see live music and shows:

1. Manzoni Auditorium Teatro

Auditorium Manzoni is a premier venue for classical music concerts, chamber music performances, and recitals.

Acoustic Excellence: The auditorium's superb acoustics provide both artists and audiences with an immersive experience.

2. Arena del Sole Theatre

Teatro Arena del Sole provides a diverse range of entertainment, from theatrical plays to live music concerts.

Check their schedule for concerts by local and international performers and bands.

3. Bentivoglio Cantina

Jazz and Blues Nights: Cantina Bentivoglio is a well-known venue that hosts live jazz and blues performances.

Intimate Setting: Sip wine or aperitivo while listening to soulful music in an intimate and pleasant setting.

4. The Estragon Club

Estragon Club is a renowned venue for live music events, with performances by both well-known and rising musicians.

Rock and Indie Music: The club's dynamic calendar includes events with rock, indie, and electronic music.

5. Congratulations, Caffè

Acoustic Music Sessions and Live Performances: Bravo Caffè is a beautiful café that conducts acoustic music sessions and live performances.

Relax with a coffee or a drink while listening to great musicians play a variety of genres.

6. The Locomotive Club

Locomotiv Club is a well-known venue for alternative music, which includes punk, rock, and experimental genres.

Live Bands and DJs: Enjoy explosive live performances and dance evenings with visiting and local bands and DJs.

7. Jazz Festival in Bologna

Annual Event: If you visit during the Bologna Jazz Festival, you'll be in for a treat.

Jazz Extravaganza: The event will showcase an all-star roster of jazz musicians from Italy and throughout the world.

8. Club Covo

Covo Club is a popular venue for indie music fans, offering live bands and themed music evenings.

Discover New Bands: This is the spot to find out about new bands and artists in your area.

Live music and concert venues in Bologna provide a diverse and dynamic selection of musical experiences, allowing you to discover different genres and enjoy the abilities of local and international musicians. Whether you enjoy classical music's refinement, jazz's lyrical rhythms, or rock and indie bands' exhilarating intensity, Bologna's music scene promises spectacular performances and unforgettable nights.

9.4 Calendar of Festivals and Events

Throughout the year, Bologna presents a bustling calendar of festivals and events that allow visitors to immerse themselves in the city's cultural, culinary, and artistic celebrations. Bologna is always buzzing with activity, from traditional religious festivals to contemporary music events. Here's a comprehensive list of some of the major festivals and events taking place in the city:

1. Prize for Art Hotels in Bologna (January)

Art and Culture: This distinguished art award honors contemporary artists and their contributions to the field of art.

The winning artists' pieces are shown at various sites throughout the city, and the award ceremony is held at Palazzo dei Notai.

2. January/February: Arte Fiera

Arte Fiera is one of Italy's leading contemporary art fairs, attracting artists, galleries, and art fans from all over the world.

Painting, sculpture, photography, and multimedia installations are among the art genres featured at the fair's artistic showcase.

3. Children's Book Fair in Bologna (April)

Literary Excellence: This well-known fair honors children's books and illustrators.

Book Exhibits and Workshops: Publishers, authors, and illustrators present their works, and various workshops and events for children and families are available.

4. Vinforum (June/May)

Vinforum is a wine and food festival that honors Italian wine and culinary traditions.

Visitors can partake in wine tastings, witness cooking demonstrations, and learn about the art of food pairing.

5. Jazz Festival in Bologna (June)

Jazz Extravaganza: This yearly jazz festival together local and international jazz performers for a series of enthralling concerts.

Concerts are held in a variety of locations throughout the city, creating a lively and dynamic jazz ambiance.

6. Ritrovato Cinema (June/July)

Cinema Ritrovato is a well-known film festival devoted to the history of cinema and the preservation of old films.

Screenings of restored and rediscovered films from various eras and countries are part of the festival.

7. Water Show in Bologna (June/July)

Bologna Water Show is a one-of-a-kind event that takes place on the city's rivers.

Water Projections: Historic building faces are transformed into canvases for hypnotic water projections and light performances.

8. The Rediscovered Cinema Under the Stars (July)

Open-Air Cinema: A continuation of Cinema Ritrovato, this event features outdoor cinema screenings in Piazza Maggiore.

Movie Magic: Watch outstanding flicks under the stars in Bologna's historic main piazza.

9. Bologna Estate (Bologna in Summer)

Summer Festivities: The Bologna Estate hosts a series of activities, concerts, and performances throughout the summer.

Summer events bring the city to life, from open-air music to street shows.

10. San Petronio's Day (October)

Festa di San Petronio is a Catholic celebration commemorating Bologna's patron saint, Saint Petronius.

Processions & Celebrations: Processions, religious services, and cultural events are all part of the celebration.

11. Bologna Motor Show (November/December)

Motorshow Bologna is one of Europe's most important car exhibitions.

Car aficionados can examine the latest models and witness thrilling live performances by professional drivers.

The schedule of festivals and events in Bologna provides numerous possibilities to interact with the city's cultural history, culinary delights, and artistic manifestations. Whether you're like modern art, classical music, Italian wine, or vintage flicks, the broad festival calendar in Bologna provides interesting experiences all year.

As we conclude our tour of the wonderful city of Bologna, we hope that this comprehensive travel guide has been a reliable companion and has opened the door to a plethora of unforgettable experiences. Bologna, a city rich in history, art, and gastronomic pleasures, has a distinct charm that enchants every visitor who strolls through its old streets and bustling neighborhoods.

Bologna unveils its secrets and stories to those who travel forth with an open heart and interested mind, from the stately Piazza Maggiore and the iconic Two Towers to the awe-inspiring Basilica di San Petronio and the hidden gems nestled away in its courtyards.

Enjoy the delectable aromas of Bolognese cuisine, the city's bustling arts and music scene, and the warmth of its local customs and traditions. Bologna has a plethora of adventures to offer, whether you're discovering the rich history at the Archiginnasio or relaxing in the tranquil Giardini Margherita.

The city's festivities change with the seasons, inviting you to join in the joyful celebrations that bring the community together. Every event, from art fairs and jazz festivals to religious processions, adds to the cultural fabric of this bustling city.

Remember that Bologna is more than just a place; it is an embrace of life itself. Take your time wandering around its lively markets, sipping cappuccino in small cafés, and basking in the kindness of the residents who welcome you with open arms.

As you bid farewell to this captivating city, may the memories you've gathered here stay with you, and may the essence of Bologna accompany you wherever your travels take you next. As the sun sets on this chapter, we hope it heralds the start of endless adventures in the world beyond.

We wish you safe travels, unforgettable experiences, and a deep appreciation for the magic that Bologna, the heart of Italy, has shared with you, with this guide as your faithful companion.

Until we meet again on your next journey, arrivederci and farewell, dear traveler.

Made in the USA
Las Vegas, NV
17 January 2024

84467939R00101